MINDFULNESS FOR STRESS & ANXIETY

Antonia Ryan

© ANTONIA RYAN 2020
WinsPress.com

While every precaution has been taken in the preparation of this book, the publisher assumes no responsibility for errors or omissions, or for damages resulting from the use of the information contained herein.

MINDFULNESS FOR BINGE EATING

Copyright © 2020 Antonia Ryan.

Written by Antonia Ryan.

Contents

Contents 2
Introduction 4
How to Download Your Guided Meditations. 13
Chapter One: Choose Freedom. 14
    Meditation 1: The Body Scan. 31
Chapter Two: Attitudes of Mindfulness 34
    Meditation 2: The Beginner's Mind Meditation. 45
Chapter Three: Attention. 47
    Meditation 3: Attention. 74
Chapter Four: Attachment and Letting Go. 77
    Meditation 4: Attachment. 97
Chapter Five: Finding Peace and Happiness 100
    Meditation 5: Peaceful Calmness 120
Chapter Six: Appreciation and Acceptance. 124
    Meditation 6: Appreciation. 142
Chapter Seven: Compassion. 145
    Meditation 7: Compassion. 174
Chapter Eight: Continuing the Journey 177
    Meditation 8: Five-Minute Mindfulness Meditation. .. 196
Appendix 1: A Brief History of Mindfulness. 198
Appendix 2: Mindful Movement. 200

- Equipment and Clothing. 200
- The Pose of a Child. 202
- Seated Forward Fold. 202
- Legs up the Wall. 204
- Tree Pose. 205
- Cat/Cow Pose. 206
- Reclined Butterfly. 207
- Standing Forward Fold 208
- Corpse Pose. 209

Appendix 3: Mindful Breathing. 211
- Equal breathing. 213
- Belly Breathing. 213

Appendix 4: Eating a Meal Mindfully. 215
Appendix 5: Self-care Activities 217
Resources 221
References 222
Acknowledgements 225
About the Author. 226

Introduction

"Now is the future you promised yourself last year, last month, last chapter. Now is the only moment you'll ever really have. Mindfulness is about waking up to this."
– Mark Williams.

***

Louise had just started another new job in a shoe shop. She had an art degree but felt she didn't have the confidence to pursue a career in the art or teaching. Louise had tried a variety of job roles but struggled to keep a job for more than a few months. Things weren't going so well in this job either. The customers terrified her, and she went to work each day with a churning stomach and heart palpitations.

Sometimes she just couldn't focus on what customers were saying or retain the information they gave her. Thoughts just seemed to unravel in her head like a messy ball of knitting wool. Overwhelming feelings of panic and nausea drowned out what people were saying to her. Louise worried about making errors and the more worried she got, the more she made mistakes. Her inability to sleep through the night wasn't helping either. She would lie awake for hours going back over her mistakes from the previous day or worrying about what she would do if she lost another job.

Louise felt like she was behind a glass screen, detached from the people and world around her. Her new colleagues were wary of her, misinterpreting her silence as a type of snobbishness. During the breaks, she would try to join in the conversation with the other staff, but by the time she had rehearsed in her head what she would say, the conversation had moved on. The more misunderstood she felt, the worse she felt. Some days she was so nauseous she couldn't eat. Her breathing was rapid and shallow and, because of lack of food and shallow breathing, she was prone to feeling faint. This made her more panicked and worried about the embarrassment of fainting in public.

Each evening she would return home alone and shut the door, dissolving into tears, feeling lower with each passing day. She retreated into her shell, shutting out the world by losing herself in TV soap operas and zombie novels.

***

"It's Monday, mum… No, it's not Saturday, Its Monday…" Rob sighed deeply as his 90-year-old mother continued to seemingly ignore what he said, continuing to ask him what day it is. He clenched his jaw and squeezed his eyes shut as tried to summon up some patience, feeling increasingly agitated.

As he held the phone to his ear, he surveyed his flat. Dirty dishes were piled high in the sink. Beer cans spilled out of the bin. His laptop was open – he had been in the middle of completing an online application form for a job. Paperwork, mostly bills, littered the table. His stomach twisted in knots and he felt like a heavy weight was bearing down on him. It was all getting too much.

"Okay, okay mum I'll ring back later. Okay. Bye" Rob groaned and put his head in his hands as he saw the application form had timed out and he would have to start all over again… A wave of despair overwhelmed him. He sat down heavily and slammed the laptop shut. It was probably a waste of time, he thought. At my age, who is going to give me a job anyway?

***

If you can relate to any of the symptoms of anxiety and stress Louise or Rob experienced, then this book will help you. We all experience stress and anxiety at some stage our lives. Knowing this might help you feel less alone. Although we cannot totally avoid these feelings, there are techniques we can use and attitudes we can adopt that can make the feelings more bearable and help us navigate ourselves towards a more comfortable experience of the world.

The Story Behind This Book.

I grew up in Northern Ireland in the 1970s and 1980s, a period of civil unrest and armed conflict known as 'The Troubles'. As a teenager, to cope with the strains of living through such a stressful time, I was attracted to meditation practices, and attitudes of mindfulness such as compassion, gratitude, acceptance, and letting go. I didn't call it mindfulness back then, but that is what it was. I genuinely believe these practices and ways of interacting with the world have benefited me hugely.

I have used mindfulness practices both professionally and personally for most of my adult life. I am a qualified social worker, teacher, and meditation instructor. I have worked for thirty years in the 'helping professions', teaching, supporting, and coaching people of all ages and backgrounds with issues such as anxiety, stress, and depression. I have used a variety of techniques and drawn from a range of disciplines. I have also worked in specialist units and hospital settings with people with anxiety disorders. Coaching people on a one-to-one basis, I have seen how these simple but effective techniques profoundly help people.

So, this book is a synthesis of my professional and personal experience. In addition, I will refer to research that backs up what you will read in this book with scientific evidence. If you are new to mindfulness, I will explain the practices. You need not know anything about mindfulness to use this book. My understanding of mindfulness is that it is essentially about keeping your attention on the present, accepting your experience of everything as it is, without pushing it away or clinging on to it.

You might associate mindfulness with Eastern religions or mystical beliefs. Although mindfulness does have its roots in the spiritual traditions of the East, as it has developed in the West it is not a spiritual practice. It has been developed into a form of treatment for stress, anxiety, depression, and addiction. Therefore, mindfulness is compatible with any faith or none. At the University of Massachusetts Medical School, American professor Jon Kabat-Zinn pioneered the use of mindfulness as a successful treatment for stress and anxiety, and since then it has become a mainstream treatment recommended by health services worldwide.

Mindfulness can help you notice and deal with emotions that are troublesome or destressing. You will learn techniques to identify subtle cues that anxiety or stress is building before it becomes overwhelming. Your self-confidence and self-belief will improve. This in turn will help you to roll with setbacks, disappointments, or perceived failures. Having a mindfulness practice will support you in establishing methods to self-soothe and comfort in ways that support your mental, emotional, and physical health. By developing healthier habits to deal with stress, anxiety, or negative emotions you will break the stress cycle. We will discuss the stress cycle later.

With a continuing mindfulness practice, you will become more resilient. You will not be knocked back or shaken so easily by life's ups and downs. You will cope with losses or disappointments. This type of resilience is not a grim 'grit your teeth and push through it' type of resilience but a type of tenacity that is based on compassion and comes from a firm, confident foundation of inner strength. The self-care habits you will build and self-awareness you will discover through your mindfulness practice will form solid pillars to support you through life's changes. You will experience your feelings, as mindfulness is not about pushing feelings away, but you will learn that the feelings will not overwhelm you.

Your quality of sleep will improve. As your base-line level of stress and anxiety drops, you will feel more relaxed and ready to settle down to a good night's sleep. In addition, your healthier methods of dealing with stress will replace habits that can undermine quality sleep such as over-indulgence with caffeine, sweets, alcohol, or over-working.

Mindfulness is ultimately about connection: connection with ourselves, our feelings, thoughts, sensations, environment, and connection with others. Therefore, your relationships with other people will improve too. Indeed, the quality of your relationships with others will serve as feedback on how you are building mindfulness practices into your daily life. Throughout the book I encourage you to reach out to others to forge and maintain connections.

If you are in any form of treatment or therapy, I recommend you share the practices you have found helpful with your therapist. The awareness and insights you gain from your mindfulness practices will no doubt enhance the effectiveness of your treatment.

How to Use this Book.

The book is divided up into eight chapters, each with a main theme. Each chapter has a guided meditation script on the relevant topic. You can download a free recording of all eight meditations in this book, read by me. (Details on how to download your recordings follow this chapter.)

You can listen to the meditations as frequently as you wish. I have had positive feedback from readers who have found the guided meditations to be very calming and supportive. These guided meditations make it easier for you to mediate, as all you have to do is settle back and listen to my voice. You will have thoughts come into your mind, this is perfectly normal, when this happens, just focus on what I am saying to you and let the thoughts go. There will be more guidance on meditation later in the book. The meditations are there to support you but if you find overwhelming feelings come up as you listen to them, take it easy. Do not force yourself to listen to the meditations. Some might appeal to you more than others, so you can repeat listening to the mediations that are supportive to you.

You can read through each of the chapters in the book at your own pace, moving along as quickly or as slowly as you wish. You might want to read though the book quickly and then re-visit the sections that you feel are most relevant to you. Alternatively, you could read a short section each day and carry out the suggested exercises. You might need to take it very slowly if you feel overwhelming emotions, so work through the book at a pace that is comfortable for you.

I suggest that you complete some writing in a journal. I propose the use of a journal for the following reasons: Firstly, the process of writing can be an outlet for turbulent feelings and help you to let go of emotions that are troublesome. Secondly committing thoughts and feelings to paper can help us see them more objectively. Thirdly, the journal can be a record of your personal journey. Reading back through it will help you see your progress or show up patterns of thought or behaviour you hadn't spotted before and lastly the very fact that you are making the effort to write something down registers to your brain that this is important, so it helps with focus and concentration. However, if journaling feels alien or uncomfortable, there are other practices you can use instead, which I will introduce in the first chapter.

Compassion is something I will talk a lot about in this book. I will encourage you to be compassionate with yourself as well as others. In-keeping with this spirit of self-compassion, please do bear in mind the following points:

Firstly, do not expect yourself to complete this book in a perfect way. You might read a section, leave it, forget to practise the suggestions, and then go back to it. That's okay. I lay the book out in a structured way for clarity but feel free to dip in and out. There is no perfect way to read the book or carry out the exercises. Keep a gentle and kind attitude towards yourself. This very act of kindness is a mindfulness practice.

Secondly, if you become aware of patterns of thinking, reacting, or behaviours that you feel needs to change, don't beat yourself up about this. You have been doing your best and you can change any unhelpful habits with a spirit of benevolence towards yourself.

Thirdly, the practice of self-compassion does not take any more time than self-criticism. Simply setting an intention to be kind towards yourself is the foundation. I will introduce practical ways to show yourself compassion but for now just adopt an attitude of care and kindness towards yourself as you embark on your mindfulness practice.

How to Download Your Guided Meditations.

To download the eight audios that accompany this book, please go to web page:

www.subscribepage.com/mindfulnessaudio1.

There is a quick email registration, then you will be directed to the downloads page. You can either listen to your audios on the web or download them to a device to use at your leisure.

When you register, you will also receive an email from me with a confirmation of the link to your downloads, which might be handy for you to refer to later. By being registered, you will have access to any updates and free resources I send out in the future. I'm sure you will want these, but you can of course unsubscribe at any time if you wish.

Just in case you have any technical problem accessing the downloads page using the method above, I have a backup system. You can also get access by sending a blank email to mindfulaudio@gmail.com. Your blank email will trigger an autoresponder that will send you the access link.

Chapter One: Choose Freedom.

"Today you can decide to walk to freedom. You choose to walk differently. You can walk as a free person, enjoying every step." – Thich Nhat Hanh.

***

The TV illuminated Louise's face, as she absorbed in the storyline of her favourite soap opera. She enjoyed losing herself in these stories about the lives of other people. They numbed out the feelings of worry and inadequacy that gnawed at her during most of her waking hours. The mobile phone flashed up an incoming call from her sister, Vikki. Louise ignored the call. She didn't want to talk to anyone tonight. Vikki would ask her about her day and Louise did not wish to re-live the humiliation of her experiences in work. The scanner wouldn't work on her till and she had dissolved into tears when the stroppy woman she was serving tutted and rolled her eyes. She would ring Vikki back to tomorrow – maybe.

This was how Louise spent most of her weekends and evenings. Going out was just too anxiety provoking. Crowds made her feel panicky, and she always worried about getting home safely. It hardly seemed worth all the effort of getting dressed up, organising taxis, and worrying about getting back home. She would usually just stand on the side-lines of the group she was with, feeling tongue-tied and left out, so

Louise just didn't bother anymore. Vikki was always trying to get her to go out, but Louise just couldn't face it.

***

As the microwave whirred around, the light from the small oven glowing in the gloom of the kitchen, Rob cast his mind back to happier days. He had enjoyed the comradery of his job at the car factory where he had worked for thirty years. As Rob cracked open another beer, he felt the familiar hurt and rage rise up again. The closure of the factory had hit him hard. That had been over a year ago and he still hadn't found another job. He took the beer into the living room, his appetite gone as his stomach lurched. The pile of bills stacked on a table in the corner, made his heart race. He just couldn't summon up the energy to tackle them. The days seemed to drift by punctuated by distressing calls from or visits to his mother. His thoughts raced ahead: he might lose the home, his mother might have an accident, he might have a heart attack…on and on his imagination conjured up scenarios of disaster and despair. As Rob considered these dire scenarios, he could feel his heart beating like a drum and he felt breathless and dizzy. Rob sat down heavily in the armchair, alarmed by the intensity of his feelings.

***

You have probably heard of the stress response. This is a term for the physical reactions our bodies make to a perceived threat. It doesn't matter what the threat is; it doesn't even matter if the threat is real or not. If we think we are under attack, our body will get ready for fight, flight, or freeze. Stress hormones will rush into the body to get us ready to run or act quickly to move out of danger. We might feel a rush of anger and lash out or we might feel numb, unresponsive and want to hide. The stress response is an ancient bodily mechanism to keep us safe. In our modern world, stress is a natural reaction to the pressure of deadlines, trying to meet the expectations of a demanding boss or relative, or worries about finances or health. We may feel like we have no control over such circumstances or life events, but we can control our *reactions* to these issues. How stress is perceived has a direct influence on how it affects health and well-being.

Kelly McGonigal is a Stanford University psychologist and lecturer. In researching studies of people suffering from stress and comparing their perceptions of stress to mortality figures, she saw a clear correlation between those who *perceived* their stress to be worse with a higher mortality rate.[1]. She has expressed this as: "It turns out that thinking stress is bad for you… is really bad for you." These studies show how our thoughts can exacerbate or ameliorate the stressful feelings we have. By allowing our bodily sensations of stress to just be without resisting them, we can make space for a calmer, less panicked reaction to these feelings. In this way, we break the unhelpful responses to a perfectly natural stress response.

By tolerating these feelings and being present with them, we can teach our brains we have faced the trigger of our anxiety and survived. It is okay. These feelings will not kill us.

Realising that these physical sensations are natural and even helpful, we can begin to feel less agitated about the sensations themselves.

Using practices such as slow, deep breathing, we help soothe and calm our nervous system. These interventions help our brains to re-wire and experience stress and anxiety differently. Instead of automatically thinking, "Oh no, here I go again, I feel dizzy, I'm going to be sick, I will faint and make a fool of myself, I feel out of control…" we can take control by rolling with these feelings rather than fighting them.

We can make space for them, allow for them, and know that they are just feelings. They will come and they will go. Our brains will experience this acceptance, and because we are not resisting, the brain will re-configure your reaction to the stress response. We can experience the stress response, see it for what it is, and choose how we respond to sensations such as a racing heartbeat or a sudden, intense feeling of anger. We can choose to experience the feelings for what they and let them go.

The stress response triggers hormones and bodily reactions that prime us for ultimate performance. This is a helpful thing. Hormones such as adrenalin and cortisol help us react promptly, to feel motivated, to act, and to be alert. McGonigal's research has shown that the pituitary gland releases oxytocin. We know oxytocin as the 'hug drug'. By releasing this hormone during stressful situations, it motivates us to seek support from others and make connections. The release of all these hormones is designed to help us deal with a crisis or an emergency. If you feel your heart beating wildly or are aware of your rapid breathing, these are just natural reactions to a situation your brain perceives to be a danger. It does not even have to be an objective, rational threat – just whatever you personally perceive to be dangerous or risky.

So, anxious or stressful feelings are not problems in themselves. Anxiety is a perfectly normal reaction to fearful events or situations. The feelings and the stress response help keep us safe and gives us the impetus to act. Therefore, the problem lies in our reaction to these feelings. There is no need to beat yourself up about this. These responses have built up slowly over time. Try to look at your thoughts and feelings with a beginner's mind today. That means looking at them afresh, with objective curiosity and not getting emotional about them. Establish a habit of regularly checking in with yourself to look at what you are feeling and thinking. See if there are any links between thoughts and feelings. This growing awareness of your thinking and habitual reactions will help you see how ingrained responses are contributing to the experience of stress and anxiety.

The scientific discovery in recent years of neuroplasticity has been an exciting breakthrough. Instead of believing that once we reach adulthood, our brains are fixed, scientists have now discovered that we can alter the neural pathways. We can strengthen areas of the brain just as we can strengthen any muscle in the body by lifting weights or doing strength training. By training our brains to think and react differently using mindfulness practices, we can reduce our perception of anxiety and stress.

An example of neuroplasticity is London taxi drivers.[2] Researchers did a study on the brains of people who had to learn where every street is in the vast city of London. In the days before in-car GPS, these would-be taxi drivers had to study the London road atlas and memorise every street, square, road, avenue, and monument in that vast city. The researchers took images of the brains of the taxi drivers before and after their period of intense study and exams to qualify them as a driver. The images showed that their brains had changed. They had made new neural connections in response to the work they had done in memorising the locations of streets in London.

This gives great hope for anyone who wishes to alter how their brain functions. With anxiety and stress, we have fallen into set ways of thinking, perceiving, and reacting to stimuli. If we can adjust these ways of reacting to the stress response, we have hope of living a calmer and happier life.

Neuroscience has proven that the parts of the brain responsible for learning and emotional regulation, namely the hippocampus and the amygdala, are affected by constant stressful thoughts. So, reacting to stress and anxiety with more stress and anxiety only makes the situation worse. It can end up being a vicious cycle that can be hard to break out of.

However, by being more aware of how we automatically respond to situations, we can break the cycle of anxious thoughts and feelings leading to yet more anxious thoughts and feelings. By interrupting the cycle, we can have more control over these troublesome sensations. In this way, we can re-wire our brains with mindfulness practices. We can train our brains to be calmer by practising mindfulness activities such as meditation, mindful walking, breathing exercises, and attending to one task at a time. By nurturing a calm and peaceful centre, you will be able to respond in a measured and less dramatic way. In addition, mindfulness practices will help you to tune into the nuances of emotions and bodily sensations before they build and end up feeling overwhelming.

You might feel perplexed by the anxiety you experience about a situation that other people seem to deal with easily or even enjoy. Disordered anxiety is when we feel intense anxiety about a situation that is not putting us in danger. It is also considered disorganized anxiety when the level of our anxiety about mildly stressful situations or events stops us from functioning. The exhilaration someone might feel about commencing a day's work might be perceived as agonizing and terrifying fear by someone else. This intense anxiety might mean they stay at home and ring in sick and eventually lose their job. One person might enjoy the hustle and bustle of a busy city street, while someone else might perceive this as sensory overload and find completely terrifying.

Now, you can practice a simple exercise to begin exploring your anxiety and stress. Try to find a quiet, comfortable place to do it. You can always read through what I suggest and do it later when it is more convenient. Recall a situation that makes you feel quite fearful or anxious. You do not need to think of something that is deeply troubling; start with something a bit easier for you. Perhaps a fear of something that might happen or feelings you have about something that you need to do but keep putting off due to anxiety. Put your hand on your heart and breath slowly. Be aware of what comes up for you about this situation and remind yourself that you have some control, you will survive. Take your time. If you feel sensations such as your breath quickening or your heart racing, just consciously slow down your breathing. This slow, deep breathing will help the heart rate slow down. By relaxing and letting go, you are making space for what is. Just look at the thoughts coming into your head with a sense of detachment. Don't get into any debate with the thoughts or criticize yourself about the thoughts, just observe them dispassionately.

By practising mindfulness techniques such as this simple exercise, you are teaching your brain that you can survive stressful thoughts. You do not have to be a victim of them. You can practice this exercise when you are feeling calm and use it as a tool to fall back on if you are suddenly assailed by stressful thoughts or sensations in real life contexts.

Re-framing responses to stress or anxiety does not mean you will never feel anxious again. As we discussed, anxiety and the bodily sensations that go with it are perfectly natural. But a reduction in disordered anxiety is a realistic goal.

***

Perhaps you feel stressed and that you have unrealistic demands placed on your time, so you work harder, trying to cram more tasks into shorter periods of time. Let's look at the example of Patricia:

Patricia always felt like there was not enough time. She felt guilty that she was at work so much and didn't have time for her daughters. She felt guilty when she handed in a project late into work. Patricia was always clock watching with a sense of panic about time moving on. She had a long mental to-do list that would be impossible to complete in the time she had. She felt compelled to have that phone call with a client as she dashed around the supermarket or respond immediately to an email on her phone while helping her daughters with their homework, or cooking while trying to check some plans for work. She never had enough time to do everything she needed to do. Patricia felt that she did not have the luxury of doing just one thing at a time.

Do you relate to Patricia? Do you feel that you have to multi-task to get everything done? Multi-tasking has a deceptive allure, as it might feel like we are getting more done, but this comes at a cost. Research conducted at Stanford University concluded that multitasking is bad for our brains.[3] Participants who completed one task at a time could complete tasks much more efficiently than those who tried to multitask. It turns out that multitasking is more about task-switching. It takes time for the brain to focus and then re-focus on another task. This delay created inefficiency and a cumulative delay in completing tasks. Constant task-switching puts more stress on the brain and can contribute to feelings of overwhelm.

Another study at London University showed that multitasking was detrimental to brain development.[4] Individuals who multitasked were shown to have slower response rates and impaired attention and focus compared to those who concentrated on one task at a time. Also, this study showed that people who thought they were effective and proficient multi-taskers were, in fact, self-deluded and were proven to be less efficient than their mono-tasking colleagues.

So, try as best you can to concentrate on one job at a time. By focusing on one task at a time, we can become absorbed in it. We can experience the calm, satisfied feeling that comes with doing a job well. We can build a powerful connection in the reward centre of our brain between the activity and the agreeable feelings we feel. That way, we will stop associating certain activities with a frantic sense of overwhelm and instead associate them with a sense of achievement and purpose. Try doing one task that you usually juggle to complete with another one – for example, cooking a meal while catching up on your emails on your laptop. Concentrate on cooking the meal and evaluate how you feel and the quality of the meal. Approach cooking the meal as a mindfulness activity and catch up on the emails later.

Tackling one task at a time is better for our mental and emotional health and is, in fact, in the long run, a much more effective way to accomplish jobs more efficiently and promptly. By multi-tasking we are putting more stress on our brains and end up feeling frazzled and overwhelmed.

***

I remember once when I had a particularly stressful period in my life, a wise friend counselled me to 'put myself into the centre of my life'. At the time I was so worried about other people and preoccupied with how they might react or behave, I disregarded my own experience of what was going on. When life gets stressful or we have anxious thoughts, it is so easy to feel like we are spinning out of control, and so we try to anchor onto external things, people, or being busy. So, pause at regular intervals, even just for a few seconds to breathe and bring your attention to what is going on for you at that given moment. Remember to direct kind thoughts towards yourself and accept what you are feeling without harsh self-judgment.

At regular intervals just pause to notice what is going on for you. Observe and experience your reactions, feelings, sensations, and habits. Noting any observations in a journal or notebook can be useful in seeing patterns. The act of writing can also help in processing difficult or strong emotions. Some people find that journaling is not helpful for them. If this is the case for you, you can practice other activities instead. You could try talking to yourself in a comforting and supportive way. Even if this 'talk' is just inside your own head, it is a way of registering and validating your experiences. Use language that feels right for you. Use words and language you would normally use, just ensure the words are kind and supportive. Talk to yourself as you would a dear friend. You could also try writing yourself a letter, listing what you have noticed about your feelings in situations that you are anxious about or feel stressed about.

A body scan is a mindfulness practice that brings our attention to the bodily sensations. (We will discuss this in more detail at the end of the chapter and a guided mediation on a body scan is coming up in the next section.) The act of doing the body scan helps you slow down and relax. Whatever you manage to do or don't do, consider the keywords of compassion and curiosity. Observe with interest and gentleness. If you forget to complete a practice, just resolve to do it the next day. Remember, you can restart your day at any time. By that I mean, if you begin to feel overwhelmed – whether that means feeling angry, distressed, or upset – you can pause, take a short break to practise slow, deep breathing, or a body scan, or have a comforting and supportive chat with yourself and then carry on with your day.

Be present. Stay in the centre of your own life. Remember that it is your attitudes that are at the heart of your mindfulness practice, not ticking body scans off your to-do list and rushing headlong back into your day. Attitudes such as willingness, gratitude, patience, letting go, acceptance, and compassion will help. We will discuss these attitudes in more detail in the next chapter.

In developing a mindfulness practice, you need to develop a routine that works for you. For many people, having some quiet time in the morning, perhaps a few minutes to read this book and then writing up your journal for five minutes or practicing some supportive and kind 'self-talk' Just taking a few moments to set a mindfulness intention for the day can be powerful, for example, 'Today I will notice when I begin to feel anxious and take a few moments to stop and breathe.' or , 'Today I will treat myself with kindness. I will allow plenty of time to get each of my tasks completed and avoid rushing.' At regular points during the day, remind yourself to be fully present in the moment – paying total attention to whatever you are doing. You can do this during any daily activity such as brushing your teeth, showering, washing dishes or when you are waiting line or just walking about.

All the guided meditations in the book will have reference to the sensations in the body. Try to build in this body awareness as you go about your daily activities. So many of us rush through the day with little awareness of what is going on below our necks. We are so focused on mental lists and chatter such as: "Remember to pick up the dry cleaning, oh and while I head there, I can stop off to pick up some groceries… what can I make for dinner tonight?" And the endless prattle goes on.

When stressful feelings or anxious thoughts assail us, we can feel spaced-out or dizzy; we might feel we are floating or that we will faint. By feeling your feet, perhaps planting them firmly on the ground and breathing well, we can give ourselves a feeling of security and support within our own body. You could say: 'Feel your feet' to yourself as a cue to be present in your own body and avoid the disconcerting light-headedness that can accompany stressful thoughts. You could also try walking around more slowly and deliberately, planting each foot purposefully on the ground, just slowing down and being more intentional with how you move can interrupt the cycle of anxious thoughts and feelings.

The Body Scan Meditation.

A body scan is a structured mindfulness practice to help get in tune with your bodily sensations. Often, we have little awareness of tension building up. It is only when we get back, neck, or shoulder pain that we realize we have been holding tension in these areas. It is more effective to prevent tension from building up in the first place. The tricky bit is remembering to stop and take a moment to be aware of how we are feeling. The body scan helps with building this awareness that hopefully will become a sort of radar we use in daily life to search for tension building up before it becomes a problem.

In terms of stress and anxiety, this body awareness can help us manage the physical sensations that accompany anxious or stressed states. We are more aware of these feelings building and can consciously exert some control over them rather than feeling that we are at the mercy of the anxiety.

You can sit in a chair, lie on the floor, or sit on the floor as you wish. You must be comfortable. With practice, you can do a body scan practically anywhere so you will need to adjust your chosen position to what is appropriate for that situation.

If sitting in a chair, ensure your feet are flat on the floor and that your back is upright and supported but comfortable and that your shoulders are relaxed and down away from your ears. You can rest your lower arms and hands on the armrests of an armchair or if you are sitting in a chair without arms rests, you can rest your hands in your lap.

If lying down, ensure that your back is flat on the floor, that you are lying on a mat or a thick rug, and use blankets and cushions as needed to feel supported and comfortable. Make any adjustments you need to before you begin. If you have lower back issues, you could try putting a small rolled-up towel under your lower back where there is a natural gap between the floor and your back. You can lie with your legs stretched out on the floor, leaving some space between your legs, and gently allowing the feet to turn out. If this is uncomfortable for your back, you can bend the knees and have the feet rest flat on the floor. If lying on the floor, ensure you are warm and not lying in a draught.

The body scan is not a test of endurance but will hopefully be something to look forward to and enjoy as a time for some true self-care.

Notes on Meditation and Breathing.

If someone is in a highly anxious state, it can be difficult for them to focus on the breath. For someone prone to anxiety, focusing on the breath can bring on a sense of panic or feelings of being out of control. For these reasons, I will focus on attention to the body sensations, especially in the initial stages. I will refer to the breath and ask you to observe it. I will encourage you to breathe slowly and deeply through your nose. I will not be asking you to control your breath or count breaths. There are some breathing strategies listed in the appendix. Use these if they are useful to you. When I refer to the breath when explaining techniques in the book or in the guided meditations, just focus on breathing slowly and deeply. You need not do anything special with the breath. Just routinely practice breathing well.

The guided meditations will help you stay focused. It is a common misconception that meditation is about emptying the mind or having no thoughts. Thoughts will come into your mind. Don't struggle with the thoughts or feel you are failing at meditation. Your mind is not your enemy. When you are aware of thoughts, you are practising mindfulness. Just don't focus on the thought or get involved with it. Let it go. There will be more on this later.

When meditating or listening to the guided meditations, settle back and make yourself comfortable as you would if you were settling down to watch television or read a book. Enjoy the meditations and relax.

So, find a comfortable place and settle back and enjoy the body scan meditation coming up next.

Meditation 1: The Body Scan.

Find a place to sit or lie down comfortably. You can sit upright in a chair or lie on a mat or bed. If your thoughts wander, bring them back to the body and the bodily sensations you are experiencing right now.

Bring your attention to the forehead. Close your eyes if this is comfortable for you, relax the jaw. Bring the attention to the throat and the back of the neck. Notice any tension you might feel.

Focus on the left shoulder, the left arm, hand, and fingers. Imagine any tension or stress flowing down over your left arm and out through your fingers. Now bring your attention to your right shoulder and to the right arm. Again, notice any tension you might feel. Imagine this moving down through the arm and out of the fingers.

Now focus on the heart area, keep your attention on this area, breathing in and expanding the whole chest cavity and down into the abdomen allowing the diaphragm to drop and make more space for the lungs to expand. Notice any tightness here. Stay with the breath in this area for a few moments. If you lose focus, bring your attention back to the breath and the body.

Next, bring your attention to the stomach area, breathing fully into the stomach allowing the entire chest and abdomen area to inflate fully. Just let the breath trickle out slowly and gradually with no force.

Now bring your focus to the back area, the upper back, the middle back, and the lower back. Have a sense of how your whole back feels. If you are aware of any tension, breathe into it and, as you breathe out, let the tension go, softening the muscles in the back.

Now focus on the area around the hips. Notice the sensations of sitting or lying. Be aware of the contact your seat area makes with the chair or floor. Notice any tension, breathe into it, and let it go.

Focus now on your left thigh, the left knee, back of the knee, calf, and shin. Have an awareness of the whole left leg. Now bring your awareness to the right thigh, the right knee, back of the knee, calf, and shin.

Shift your focus to the left foot, front of the foot, heel, sole, and ball of the foot; be aware of any sensations or lack of sensations in the toes. Feel how the footrests on the floor. If barefoot, feel how the air moves around the foot. Now bring your attention to the right foot, the front of the foot, heel, sole, and ball of the foot. Be aware of how the toes feel or be aware of any lack of feeling in the toes.

Have a sense of being grounded, a sensation of heaviness, Feel any slight movement of air around the body or parts of the body. Be aware of the entire body. Focus on breathing well and keeping your focus on the complete body and breath.

After a few moments bring your attention back to the room, you are in. With your eyes still closed, imagine the room in your mind's eye. Be aware of any sounds in the room or close to the room. Open your eyes, stretch slowly, and move on with your day.

Chapter Two: Attitudes of Mindfulness

Sitting at her small kitchen table, Louise read the text her sister Vikki sent last night. 'Oh no,' Louise groaned inwardly. Vikki wanted her to join her on an evening course. Louise sipped on her coffee, contemplating another agonising day at the shop. Vikki, a confident staff nurse, three years her senior, seemed to approach Louise as a project to get fixed. This was her latest attempt to sort out Louise. Vikki had been pestering her about this course for months, insisting it would help Louise break out of her anxiety.

Louise hated the idea of being in a group. She had spent most of her life avoiding these sorts of situations. She was sure there was something about her that people didn't like, but she wasn't sure what. A vague, nagging sensation that she just wasn't good enough seemed to dog her.

Louise exchanged a few messages with her sister, who reassured Louise that, no, she didn't have to say anything at the course if she didn't want to and, yes, Vikki would go with her, so Louise grudgingly agreed to go. Maybe Vikki would get off her back now and leave her alone.

***

Rob walked away from the doctors' surgery. He had asked for some medication to help him deal with his insomnia, lack of appetite, and constant thoughts of future personal disaster. But instead, the young, enthusiastic doctor had given him a leaflet about mindfulness and invited him to join a group. This was not what Rob had expected but had agreed to give it a go. His mobile phone vibrated in his pocket and a picture of his mum flashed up on the screen. Rob sighed as he took the call, suddenly remembering he had agreed to visit her today but due to lack of sleep he had forgot all about it. 'I am such a loser,' he thought to himself, 'What an idiot...'

***

If we can incorporate attitudes of mindfulness such as compassion, acceptance, or gratitude in how we operate in the world and in relationships with ourselves and others, mindfulness becomes less about a practice and more about who we are. It's a choice we can make every morning: do I want to be more compassionate, patient, present, willing, accepting, forgiving, and grateful?

Compassion, including self-compassion, is at the heart of any mindfulness practice. Many of us judge ourselves more harshly than our worst critics, and we become our own worst enemies. Take a moment to consider your self-talk. Think about what you say to yourself or what you call yourself if you make a mistake or think you have made a mistake. Think about how your self-talk affects your feelings of anxiety or stress. When you catch yourself running a harsh, critical commentary in your head, try to replace it with a nurturing, kind voice. You could recall a parent, teacher, or relative who has been a supportive mentor and think what they would say to you.

Consider this particularly when things have not gone according to plan. Do you always think it must be your fault? What names do you call yourself? Do you give yourself any slack for fatigue, distraction, overwhelm, lack of information, or for just being human?

Equally, think about your reactions to the perceived mistakes or errors of other people. Do you react or respond? Do you immediately act on your initial feelings of irritation, aggression, or impatience or do you take a moment to consider the other person's perspective? Imagine how the world could be if we all nurtured a spirit of compassion for ourselves and others.

In Asian languages, the words 'mind' and 'heart' are used interchangeably. Therefore, mindfulness could be understood as 'heartfulness'. This makes a lot of intuitive sense because by consciously integrating attitudes of mindfulness, we become more connected with others. This in turn lifts us out of a sense of isolation or being different. The feelings of stress or anxiety we experience are part of the human experience and we are not strange, odd, or somehow defective – we are just human.

The attitudes are the tools you can use to practise in the real world. Practising (and that means sometimes failing at) these attitudes is like any other skill – we need to practise it. We can learn from our mistakes and move on. Such efforts will lift us out of the prison of negative self-belief which can feed anxiety and stress. By looking outward with pure motives and intentions, we can navigate through life's challenges with more serenity and mental peace.

I talk a lot about compassion in this book, and in chapter seven we will discuss it in more detail, but what exactly is compassion and how do we practise it? Many people think of compassion as an emotion or a feeling, but it is more of a process. The first step in this process of compassion is to be aware of what is going on for you, and noticing your own thoughts, sensations, and feelings with a kind heart. Be present in your own life. Experience fully what is happening in any one moment.

The next stage of compassion is being in tune with other people, feeling empathy, and human identification. Listening carefully to other people is an act of compassion. The Chinese character for listening includes five elements: the ears, the eyes, you, me, and heart. This is a visual reminder of how we can listen actively to others, by engaging not just the ears and eyes, but also connecting with the heart. The act of being fully present and in tune with another person is a mindfulness practice in compassion.

The last stage of the process is wishing the best for that person (and ourselves) or intending to relieve their suffering. This can be a practical action or, if we cannot take a practical step, we could make a sincere wish that their suffering is alleviated.

Compassion reminds us of the deep bond we have with others. Einstein referred to this when he talked about the self-imposed prisons of thinking we are separate from each other. He urged people to: 'Widen our circle of compassion to embrace all living things.'

Acceptance is another attitude that is an active process. We are choosing to accept what is going on in the present moment. We don't have to like it or force ourselves to enjoy it, but we can make space to allow for whatever situation or experience it is.

The next stage is letting go of the outcomes and letting life unfold. We need to avoid playing mental movies in our head of how things should unfold. Just because you want something to happen in a certain way with a particular result, it is easy to believe that this is how things should be, and we become unhappy if life chooses a different outcome. If you let go of the outcomes, you are more able to roll with life's unpleasant surprises, so you don't get hurt. Moreover, life's surprises are sometimes welcome. If you are not wedded to a certain outcome, you will see when life is handing you an unexpected opportunity and take full advantage of that.

Acceptance is not resignation. You can take positive action. Taking positive action is better than staying stuck in negative action such as feeling or acting angry, fearful, and frustrated. When we accept the present moment, we allow for more possibilities in the situation and a lighter energy of hope, possibility, and choice.

Powerful emotions such as fear, anxiety, resentment, and anger can feel almost impossible to let go of. Resentment or anger – especially if it feels like righteous anger –can go around and around in our heads, burning up good energy like a greedy flame. Holding on to resentment has been likened to drinking poison and hoping the other person dies. Yet, the only person resentments hurt is us.

Practising tolerance, acceptance, and compassion with a situation that evokes anger, fear or resentment can help. Taking the person or situation out of your head and into your heart might work. In practical terms, that means letting the angry, worried, fearful, or resentful thoughts go; and instead of ruminating on past injustices, fears, what-ifs, or what-might-have-beens, focus on your heart and channel the emotional energy of the situation away from the head and into the heart. In this way, you are acknowledging how important this situation is or has been to you. You are not dismissing it, but you are redirecting it to a place where you will be less mentally bothered by it.

In addition, trusting your heart with this person or situation will soften any harshness, disappointment, judgment, or anger that might surround the situation. Above all, accept that letting go is a process. Sometimes it's a lengthy process. There is not usually a once-and-for-all dramatic occurrence. We will discuss more ways of letting go of troubling thoughts, feelings, or memories as the book progresses.

To illustrate the benefits of letting go, I can give you a personal example of how this works. I have a close relative who has struggled with some issues over the years. I dearly wanted to have a friendly relationship with them. I tried hard to be supportive, kind, and attentive. However, often this person shouted at me, criticized me for minor mistakes, and behaved in a rude and brusque manner. Whenever I saw a missed call from them, my heart would sink. I dreaded speaking with them. After some thought, I realized that I needed to let go of the illusion that I would ever have a comfortable, mutually supportive, and respectful relationship with them. I am still in contact with them but have cut down on any social obligations and keep contact minimal. I have worked on letting go of the idea that we could be friends and accepted that this is just how it is. This person is in my heart but not my head. I need not get upset or bothered by their behaviour now as I have let it go.

We can find that when we let one thing go, and then something else pops up. That's being human. Keep working on letting go as a continual work in progress. There is more on letting go in chapter four.

Non-striving is an attitude that can alleviate anxiety dramatically. Non-striving is sailing with the wind rather than rowing furiously against it. We can have a plan or a destination, but we don't have to push so hard. We can act and do the steps to get to where we are going, but we need not overstretch or overwork and stress ourselves out. It is about yielding rather than opposing the flow of life. You can only experience the flow of life in the present moment. In martial arts, a key concept is to yield to overcome.

In relating to others, non-judging is part of acceptance and compassion. If you are with someone you accept them just as they are at that moment. We don't get hung up on what we don't like or focus on aspects of their personality or appearance they should change. You are present with them, in the here and now, just as they are. This includes yourself. If you could free yourself up from the fear of your own or other people's judgements think how free you could be to be who and what you want to be. Fear of other people's poor opinion of us can paralyse us because it limits growth and creative endeavour.

By all means, ask for and accept feedback, but unsolicited opinions are the business of other people. When I talk about judging I mean the harsh judgement that has undertones of negative criticism, blame, and shame. We can use our discretion and intelligence to judge that a situation or person may not be safe for us. We can use our intellect to give useful feedback on a piece of work or a project to help improve it or extend skills.

Stay in the centre of your own life and don't get too caught up in the judgements of others. Remind yourself that their opinions belong to them and are none of your business.

The 'inner critic' is that voice in your mind that is judgemental and critical. It will feed you a constant stream of critical observations. Listening to this inner critic will rob you of your peace of mind and self-esteem. You can choose whether you tune into the inner critic. You can replace the inner critic with the inner nurturer, or you can just watch the thoughts dispassionately, choosing not to attach any importance to what it is saying. Someone I knew used to replace their inner critic with the voice of a comical character (the 'Old Lady' from Monte Python). The voice was so silly and ridiculous it took the sting out of what the inner critic was saying. Be aware of your own 'inner critic' and do not get entangled in harsh self-judgements – see them as just 'thoughts' and let them go.

Gratitude is powerful, especially when you are feeling down. If you are having an unpleasant day, or perhaps going through a tough time in your life, you may feel that you have nothing to be grateful for. But there is always something. Take a few moments now to think of a few things you are grateful for. If you ruminate on the negatives in your life, you will probably just find more negativity. Gratitude breaks the negative downward spiral.

If any of these attitudes feel beyond you now, just be willing to let them into your consciousness. Most of them are part of a process. Keep an open and curious mind and be willing to try out some ideas. Play about with the concepts, try listening to a guided meditation, reflecting on an attitude, journaling about it, or practising focusing on an attitude as you go about your day-to-day life and just see what happens.

Be open to possibilities.

Be willing to change and see your life situation and who you are in a unique light.

Adopting these attitudes will take time and practice. Just do what you can, a little every day, consistency is key. All the attitudes become easier to remember and to apply to your life when you are fully present in each moment.

The most important thing when you close this book is to practise the attitudes, to *be* the attitudes. But be patient and allow for lots of slipping, sliding, and mistakes. Progress, not perfection.

Begin nurturing curiosity and warm-heartedness towards yourself as you go through your usual activities. Use all your senses to be present in the moment. Just notice how you do things daily. Stop at various points during the day and think about how you feel. Even if you don't know the answer, just ask: how am I feeling right now? Notice the first thoughts that come to mind in the morning when you wake up. Notice what sorts of events, people, and places that trigger any feelings of anxiety or stress. How does this manifest itself? Perhaps in feelings of tension, butterflies in the tummy, headaches, or heart palpitations? Just observe yourself, your feelings, reactions, thoughts, sensations, and habits.

The 'beginner's mind' is an attitude of mindfulness that is a gift no matter what stage you are on your mindfulness journey. Perhaps you truly are a beginner in the literal sense. If so, see this as something to help enhance your dive into mindfulness. Bring this sense of curiosity and newness into all areas of your life. Let go of old assumptions. Have a sense of seeing yourself, your environment, and the people in your life, with the eyes and mind of a beginner. Nothing is ever the same from one day to the next. This moment today is unique and always unfolding. Experience the freshness of each moment with a beginner's mind.

Meditation 2: The Beginner's Mind Meditation.

Settle yourself onto a chair or lie back on a mat. Ensure your feel supported, warm and that you can sit for at least five minutes comfortably.

Bring your awareness to the points of contact your body makes with the chair or mat.

Let the breath settle into a steady regular rhythm. There is no need to change or alter the breath. Just ensure you are breathing slowly and deeply through the nose. Be aware of the air entering the nostrils and leaving the nostrils. Just watch without judgment. Let the jaw relax a little, let the eyelids drop closed or soften the gaze.

Thoughts will come. Don't struggle with them and don't engage with them. If you have a jumble of thoughts just look at them without emotion, they are just thoughts. They will come and they will go. Take a breath and on the out-breath purposefully let the thoughts go.

Keep your focus on the words in this meditation, on your breath, and on your body. Has the jaw tightened up again? How are your shoulders? Try dropping the shoulders a little. Continue to breathe steadily and be a watcher of yourself.

Be curious. Imagine you are exploring this inner world of your sensations for the first time. Be aware of a sense of space inside your body, breath into it, allowing for a full inflation of your lungs. Enjoy any moments of stillness between thoughts, no matter how short or fleeting they are.

Recall the sensations and feelings you might have when embarking on a novel project with passion and interest. Focus on the feelings that go along with being a beginner, a learner. The excitement and thrill of starting something fresh and the anticipation of unfamiliar experiences.

Every day is a new beginning. We can bring this attitude of the 'beginner's mind' to each day, each moment. We can bring this attitude of curiosity, willingness, and openness to each interaction with others and to ourselves. We can see situations in our life with a fresh eye, a newness and freshness that lifts us out of the routine and automatic ways of perceiving and reacting to our reality.

As you go through your day, be the observer of yourself, your environment, and others as if you see them all for the first time.

Bring your attention back to the points of contact your body makes with the chair or mat. Deepen the breath a little, move the hands and feet and bring your awareness back to the room you are in. Open your eyes and look around with a sense of seeing the room for the first time. Look at the colours, shapes, and textures of the objects in the room. Let your eyes rest on one object and really look at it as if for the first time. Be aware of anything new that you see in the room or about the object you choose. After a few minutes stretch your arms up, take a breath and carry on with your day.

Chapter Three: Attention.

"The best way to capture a moment is to really pay attention. This is how we cultivate Mindfulness. It means knowing what you are doing." Jon Kabat-Zinn.

***

Louise scanned the shoe boxes with her eyes, desperate to find the correct size quickly. She felt the familiar feeling of panic well up from the pit of her stomach, making her feel queasy and constricting her chest. As usual she was aware of the clock ticking and the customer waiting downstairs. 'Why am I so slow? What's wrong with me?' Louise looked away from the wall of shoes boxes for a second and took a long, deep breath as she focused momentarily on the small square of sky she could see through the window of the storeroom. Sensing the panic subside, she re-focused her gaze on the shoebox labels and sighed with relief as she caught sight of the correct size. Louise returned to the customer with a smile, feeling more confident than she had done since she started this job. She was amazed at how slowing down, breathing, and focusing could be so powerful, but it seemed to be working.

***

"You called me Stan. It's Rob, mum."

"Did I?" Rob's mother looked at him quizzically. "I know you're not Stan, he's been dead for twenty years!" She carried on, relating her latest disagreement with her neighbour. Rob tried hard to pay complete attention to what she was saying. He had been attending the course recommended by his doctor. Last night, the teacher on the course had listened sympathetically as he tearfully discussed his worry, frustration, and feelings of powerlessness over his life, especially his mother and his work situation. It had all felt so overwhelming. Today, he was trying to pay attention to what was going on and trying to tune out of all the worrying thoughts that prophesied disaster, as his teacher had advised. It helped to keep his focus on what was in front of him. He began to feel calmer and less rattled by his mother's forgetfulness and confusion. He nodded as he sipped his tea and listened to her.

***

Our society as it has evolved is making it harder to pay attention to the present. There is nothing wrong with checking the news or being entertained. However, when this is done without intention or thought, we are losing out on the present moment. We must be intentional in how we pay attention because what we pay attention to has profound effects on how we feel and what we think. If our attention span is short and we jump from one thing to another in rapid succession, we will feel stressed.

Part of the definition of panic is 'unthinking behaviour'. In Britain there is an expression to describe panicky, pointless behaviour: running around like a headless chicken. When we are not engaged with our thoughts and reacting in old, conditioned ways, such as constantly checking our phones, jumping on Facebook, and scrolling through the news, the uncomfortable feelings of panic or fear get multiplied. So, paying attention to our thoughts and what is going on for us helps us to engage with rational, calm, and purposeful behaviour. Behaving in this way makes us feel calmer and sets up a positive cycle of being aware, engaging in intentional action and in turn feeling calmer.

In our modern world we can be constantly distracted, our thoughts scattered, and our connections with others weakened. Have you ever been with someone who was constantly checking their phone or computer? How often do you get distracted by Facebook, Instagram, or the news? If you suddenly find yourself picking up your phone for the tenth time in an hour and you aren't sure why you picked it up in the first place, you have probably done picked up the phone on autopilot.

Autopilot is the technology that keeps an aircraft on course without the intervention of the pilot. It has come to refer to those occasions when we fulfil actions without thinking or being fully aware of what we are doing. For example, how many times have you driven home on a familiar route, perhaps from work, and not even been aware of the journey? You got home safely and had used the gears, steering wheel, and controls effectively. You had slowed, stopped, and taken off again as necessary. You had followed signs, made turns, and stopped at red lights, but you have little conscious memory of doing all these complex tasks. That's autopilot. Perhaps on a day off, you set off in the car only to inadvertently and mistakenly take the road to work or your children's' school because that's the route you take most days. You did it on autopilot. Those of us with routine jobs that have a lot of repetition might fall into the habit of autopilot because we are undertaking familiar tasks.

Autopilot starts as a useful tool for learning. Imagine if we had to re-learn routine behaviours every day? How inconvenient it would be is we had to think about how to get out of bed, how to put one foot in front of the other to walk, how to brush our teeth and so on. We can learn habits so well that our brains register nothing new or out of the ordinary, so we can perform tasks without even thinking about them. We become 'habituated'.

You might think this habituation is a helpful thing because of how tedious and time-consuming it would be to have to re-learn mundane tasks every day. Learning a skill, whether it is how to walk, ride a bicycle, play the piano, drive a car, or operate machinery is all helpful. The brain has linked the habits to create learning. We know a lot now about brain plasticity and how neural pathways are created. We looked at that in the first chapter. Our habits and learning can change the physical matter of our brain. The problems arise when the habits become so automatic that we proceed without thought or attention to the task in hand. When anything happens that is unusual while we are cruising along on autopilot, we react rather than respond.

Reacting and responding are different. When we give a response in any situation, it is thoughtful, measured, and considered by our rational selves as appropriate to a situation. However, when we react, it is usually 'shooting from the hip', a quick, thoughtless, automatic reaction that may have undesired consequences. Consider this scenario:

Max was driving to work along his usual route. He was late and felt wound up, as getting out of the house that morning had been a nightmare. He hated Mondays anyway, but today was shaping up worse than usual. It was a cold, grey, wet, and the first Monday in January. The weather would have been enough to dampen his spirits on any day. But on top of that, he was running late, as he had misplaced his keys that morning. He had put them down absent-mindedly when he got in the previous night. It had been a scramble to find them.

His thoughts turned towards the presentation he had to give to his boss and senior colleagues that morning. He felt ill-prepared and was mentally rehearsing his speech, recalling his PowerPoint slides. Suddenly a lorry blasted their horn at him. It jolted Max out of his ruminations and he automatically blasted his horn back. Then he realized that he had been drifting into the inside lane without even being aware of it. Max quickly readjusted his position and dropped back, indicating to move back into the lane correctly. He felt shaken and breathed out slowly, trying to calm his pounding heart and shaking limbs.

Do you identify with Max?

Reacting on autopilot can be stressful. Often, when we react in anger, hurt, or shock, we react in ways which deep down we know are not ideal. We can either get into an argument and hold our corner or slink off feeling ashamed of our thoughtless and inappropriate response. Neither outcome is satisfactory and creates stress in our lives.

Let's go back to Max to think further about what is happening:

Max often drives to work without being able to recall any details of the journey. Although he is only in his thirties and considers himself to be a reasonably fit guy, he often feels stiff and achy as he gets out of the car. His muscles seemed to have tensed up without him being aware of it. He often feels tired and has an urge to yawn widely. Not a brilliant way to start the day.

Like many people, Max breathes in short, shallow breaths that are confined to the chest cavity. The parasympathetic nervous system interprets this as Max being under pressure. So, he is high on the stress scale even before anything happens.

Perhaps you are like Max and fall into a state of autopilot on familiar driving routes to work or school. Maybe you perform your job in this state. You might go about your daily activities, like cleaning the house or shopping, on autopilot.

I remember some years ago, I was working abroad. I had a long commute to work on a busy motorway. The driving conventions in the country were not what I was used to. I also had to be on alert in case I drifted onto the wrong side of the road, as I had been used to driving on the other side for all my adult life. I found the journey stressful. Often, I would get out of the car at my workplace after the forty-five-minute drive and find that I felt light-headed and tense. I realized I was breathing shallowly into the top part of my chest. I also noticed that my shoulders had got higher and higher, closer to my ears, clenched tightly. Does this sound familiar to you?

Going about our daily lives in this state can bring on the sensations of anxiety or fear. At the very least it robs us of joy. It takes away the colour, vibrancy, and texture of daily life. We confine ourselves to a dull, monochrome existence. No wonder then that we might feel stressed or lacking in vitality or happiness.

Many people spend their lives in a limbo state of anhedonia, an inability to enjoy life. The days pass in a cheerless but tolerable procession of activities, tasks, and commitments. There is no sense of genuine excitement or happiness. Shaking ourselves out of autopilot can be the first step along the path back to our natural state of contentment and peace, open to the delights that life has got to offer.

Take a few moments now to consider at what times in your life you drift into autopilot. When we are in autopilot, our programmed conditioning takes over. The program might be feeding us thoughts such as 'this feels unsafe' or 'you will make a fool of yourself' or 'I can't cope'. Therefore, by breaking the habit of autopilot, you can begin chose which program you are operating on. You can choose self-compassion or gratitude or acceptance.

Reflect on how you pay attention. What do you give the most attention to? How intentional are you in giving attention to the significant people in your life? How much attention to you give the news or Netflix? There is nothing wrong with these activities, but just be curious about how much time screen-based activities are taking up in your life. Is this what you want? No one is telling you what to do but consider what you want. It is your life. If you realize you are spending too many of your waking hours looking at a screen, don't be hard on yourself, just set some limits on how you use your laptop or phone.

When you pay attention to your thoughts, you might notice how many opinions come flooding into your mind. You will see you have opinions and judgements about everything. Try not to get caught up in making judgements about your judgements. We can still cultivate discernment, clarity, wisdom, and understanding. We can navigate our way through judgments. Make choices you feel are more healthful and supportive.

We need to focus on *what* we are paying attention to and *how* we are doing it.

When you note how you spend the bulk of your time and what you give your attention to, be compassionate with yourself. If you need to make changes, do them because you want to, not because you feel you must. Be willing to try unfamiliar things. Be present in your own life. If you have an indulgent afternoon of back-to-back movies on a rainy Saturday, fully immerse yourself and enjoy it. Pay attention to the feelings of cosiness and pleasure. However, if you do this *every* afternoon because you don't know what else to do and you feel restless, bored, and distracted, perhaps it's time to do something different.

***

Human perception and memory can be notoriously unreliable. Ask any police officer or legal professional. People's memories of the same incident can differ remarkably in the details they notice or miss out entirely. This is no surprise. The hippocampus is the part of the brain principally associated with memory learning and with emotion, and powerful emotion can either heighten the memory or obliterate it. If we are experiencing panic or anxiety, we will not take on board fresh information or learn easily. Our perception will be skewed.

Mindfulness exercises often focus on what we can experience through our five senses, with techniques anchored in noticing what you can hear, see, smell, touch, and taste. This is a useful starting point to become more aware of our environment and how we are feeling and responding to the stimuli we are exposed to.

Our perception as human beings goes far beyond the five senses. Have you ever been focused on a task and sensed someone behind you, and you turn around and someone is there? You haven't heard them or seen them, but you just sense that they are there? Or perhaps you sense someone looks at you and, even though you initially did not see the person, you look around and you spot the person looking your way.

Cortical blindness is a thought-provoking phenomenon. People who are technically blind – that is the optical nerves are destroyed – can 'see' whether you are raising your left hand or your right hand. They are aware of how many fingers you are holding up. Psychologists have termed this 'body mapping'. Even though the person cannot use the optic nerves to see in the conventional sense, they can discern information through their bodily senses.

I refer to this phenomenon to highlight that we are much more sensitive to our environment and other people than we might initially think based on what we believe we know from our five senses. Our senses and nervous system are delicately tuned instruments that make millions of minor adjustments to keep us safe and well. By realizing this, it is even more important to put ourselves into situations that will be of optimum benefit to our sensitive bodies and minds.

In terms of anxiety and stress, this realization can be a comfort in the sense that we have answers as to why we feel so overwhelmed and frazzled: it is because of the sensitivity of our nervous system. You can then apply more understanding and compassion to the reactions your body and mind make.

Take, for example, supermarket shopping. For some people, shopping in a supermarket provokes extreme anxiety. If we look at the typical supermarket environment, we can see why. They are far from the natural environment our bodies feel comfortable with. The lights and climate control system feel very artificial. They can be crowded. We might feel under pressure to make quick decisions. We might feel overwhelmed by too many choices, and so on.

We are not under any threat or danger, but we are simply overstimulated by an artificial environment. This knowledge can help free up mental space to accept your feelings and make some allowances for them. You are not weird. You need not feel out of control or panicked about perfectly natural human responses. However, perhaps your situation is hampering you to such a degree that what most people consider normal behaviour is not possible for you.

You might remember in Chapter 1 we talked about the stress response and how we can reconfigure neural pathways in the brain. We will revisit those ideas. We will look at how we can avoid panicking about panic and have a sense of some acceptance around these uncomfortable feelings.

Make room for acceptance of your feelings. Allow for them. Don't be harsh with yourself. See them as natural reactions that may have somehow gone awry. By accepting them, you are gently bringing your feelings back into alignment with the present moment, and in the present moment, there is no danger or threat.

You may recall we looked at the sensations associated with the stress response: feeling light-headed, a racing heart, nausea, or trembling. These sensations are very akin to feelings of excitement. We can reframe our feelings as excitement. However, when in the grip of disordered panic, this is easier said than done.

Using our mindfulness techniques to create greater awareness of bodily sensations, we make space for a fresh perspective. By grounding ourselves and breathing deeply and calmly, we can lift ourselves out of this cycle of panic – the cycle of feeling the sensations of panic and then panicking because we feel panicked.

Over time, we might have built up a bank of unhelpful or unsatisfactory responses to feelings of stress or anxiety. We might completely avoid situations. But avoidance diminishes your life experience. If we avoid close personal relationships, for example, that truly will rob us of the intimacy, trust, companionship, and closeness such a relationship can bring to our lives. You might use excessive alcohol, social media, blame, shame, or addictive behaviours to avoid situations that make you feel stressed or panicked. But when you do that, your world shrinks.

Today we will think about how you can re-frame your thoughts before you become anxious.

Techniques such as visualisation, progressive relaxation, and guided meditation can all help. Try rehearsing a situation that makes you feel anxious in your imagination, noticing your reactions and accepting them. You are training your brain to realize it is okay to feel this way. It won't kill you. These are just feelings. They will pass. You can rehearse techniques that you know will help soothe you in the imagined situation such a slow, steady breathing, repeating a word such as 'peace' or 'calm', or holding a small object such as a pebble. In your imagination, direct your attention to the less anxiety-provoking aspects of the situation; for example, keeping your attention on one of your senses that is not triggering.

This means that when you are really in the situation, your trained brain will recognize the scene, recognize the feelings, and remember that it was all okay. Also, when in the situation, you can recall what helped you when you visualised it. By habitually practising guided meditations and the body scan, you are re-setting your nervous system to operate from a calmer base. You will experience what it means to feel more peaceful, and you can take these feelings with you into situations you feel might trigger your stress or anxiety.

In helping prepare yourself for situations that provoke feelings of anxiety or stress, you can use a technique called 'anchoring'. You could use a word, a small gesture, or small object to anchor your mind back to a calm state. For example, if when calm and at peace – perhaps after a body scan or guided meditation – you might spend a few moments quietly breathing well and focusing on the word 'peace' or 'calm'. Then, when you go into the situation which you find challenging, you recall the word 'peace' or 'calm' to anchor your feelings.

You could build the same association using a small gesture, such as touching the tips of your index figure and the tip of your thumb on one hand. This will take you back to the experience you have of feeling calm and at peace. You could do this also with a small object in your pocket, such as a small pebble or keyring charm. You touch the object, and it reminds you of the calm and peaceful feelings.

By taking the time to read about how to break the stress response, doing a guided meditation, and observing thoughts and sensations you are getting your body and brain to operate from a solid base of calm and balance. Think of a lake that is deep and still. When the wind whips up, it only ruffles the surface of the water; it does not disturb it on a deeper level. Imagine you are this deep, calm lake that is not overly troubled by the challenges life throws at you.

Moving, speaking, and breathing more slowly will lower the heart rate, reduce the stress hormones raging through the body, and reduce the build-up of tension in the muscles. Also, by applying mindfulness attitudes such as compassion, acceptance, patience, and letting go, you will respond to irritations, stressors, or challenges with more equanimity and calm.

If your life circumstances are making your feel stressed, you might feel that you have little control over what is going on. This perception of lack of control can induce fearful feelings. For example. if you are a single parent, working two jobs to make ends meet, you will feel stress. You might feel that you have no choices. I have been in life situations in which I have felt very stressed and burdened by life circumstances. However, we can exert some control over the things we focus on and pay attention to, the language we use, the choices we make, the attitudes we bring to a situation, the people we spend our free time with, the material we read, watch, or listen to, our level of acceptance or resistance to how things are, how we spend our free time, how we tend to our health, food, smoking, alcohol, and we can chose whether we drift along aimlessly on autopilot or live with intention and focus.

Think about how you spend your time and what you pay attention to, consider the choices you make with a spirit of compassion. This is not about assigning blame. Some practical situations in your life might feel intolerable. But think about what you can do to re-frame your attitudes and perspective. Think about what you do have control over.

We have looked at what we can do to help ease the stress and anxiety we are experiencing. By taking back some control, we can avoid feeling victimized by these natural responses.

The following are things that you can do to avoid feelings of stress or anxiety building up: Get into the habit of doing an informal body scan regularly at points during the day to check in with yourself, to build up a steady ongoing awareness of how you are feeling in your body. When you sense tension or stress, feel your feet, get grounded, and slow down your breathing. Pay attention to what you are doing and avoid multi-tasking, deliberately slow down your movements, speech, and breath.

Earlier we talked about using visualization to help prepare you for a stressful situation. You can also make a very practical plan for how you will tackle an event that might induce anxiety or panic by planning. By formulating a plan of action and then letting the worry go, you can free yourself up to give the present moment your full attention.

Using the example of the supermarket trip, let's break down each aspect of shopping into small, manageable steps:

Plan. Write a list and only visit areas of the shop you need to go to. They usually place fresh healthy produce on the outer perimeters of the shopping aisles and the more processed food in the middle aisles, so perhaps only visit the outer edges of the shop. This will avoid feeling trapped in the middle of the store and avoid being tempted by high sugar food that can exacerbate sensations of anxiety. Go with a supportive friend or family member. Plan the maximum amount of time you can tolerate being in the supermarket. Also, have an exit plan, just in case you begin to feel overwhelmed.

By being present with each step of your plan, you can feel that you have some control over these overwhelming feelings. Make a plan that has smaller steps if you need to.

That's fine. Do what is good for you. Celebrate each small victory. Allow for setbacks.

If you take this approach, make a plan that breaks down the cause of your panic into tiny, baby steps. Don't rush it. Put the plan together with the utmost gentleness and compassion for yourself. Celebrate every little gain, no matter how small or how insignificant it might seem to someone else. These are your feelings and experiences. You need to start with where you are at.

Approach your plan with a sense of willingness to try something new.

If you are struggling with even making a plan to overcome your anxiety around a particular event or situation, just be willing to consider it. You need not do anything else just yet. Your plan is just a plan. You can decide when to carry it out.

When designing a plan, chose an easy action. Stick with it and observe your reactions. If you feel panic, ground yourself, stand tall, breathe, and feel. As you experience your bodily sensations, do so with the attitude of a detached observer if you can.

To illustrate how using this approach can work for chronic stress, I would like to share a personal story. Some years ago, I worked in a stressful job. The client group was young people with autism and challenging behaviour – which included biting, scratching, and hitting – so I had constant background stress that I could be physically hurt.

I had to work twenty-four-hour shifts and was away from home overnight two or three times a week. I had a management position, so I was responsible for stressed staff. I often had to react quickly in a crisis and had very demanding situations to deal with. I lived in a rural area with few alternative job options, and I had a large mortgage. I felt stressed continually. I also felt extremely low about my life, feeling trapped.

Through my mindfulness practice, I identified the stressed feelings and could use meditation, talking to my husband and friends, and long walks in the countryside to cope with the ongoing stress. I tried to change what I had some control over. For example, I offered mindfulness sessions to the staff or practised meditations when I had a break. I also made sure I booked regular holidays and made the most of any weekends I had.

However, I knew I would need to make major changes due to the ongoing stress of this situation. I planned. It took three years of downsizing, minimising possessions, and doing some re-training; but at the end of this time, I could sell the house, pay off the mortgage, and move abroad. Today I have a vastly different life.

Initially, I took small steps to change what I could and downsize in small easy stages. I enlisted the support of my family. I made plans for other career options and followed these through. All this took time, patience, and preparation. On the tough days at work, I would think of my plan and it helped me to cope and feel less stressed about my situation.

I made sure I built in self-care along the way with the holidays and trips at weekends.

The positive feedback you get when you achieve one step, no matter how small, will motivate you to move forward in conquering the anxiety that is holding you back.

***

Fear is a perfectly rational response to a dangerous situation. We have looked at how mindfulness practices help us be aware of our feelings and sensations. We have considered the importance of feeling them and sitting with them. This trains the brain to realize that the feeling of fear or panic associated with a certain event, place, person, or thing is manageable. You survived. The brain reconfigures new neural pathways, so the next time you encounter the fearful thing or event, the feelings will lessen in their intensity. This takes time and gentle effort.

When we are in a state of panic, we often find it hard to focus. We might forget things. We might feel that the grasp we have on our thinking is tenuous. This makes us feel even more out of control and intensifies feelings of panic.

Anything could trigger the feeling: seeing a certain expression on your boss's face, a critical email, a social event. Whatever the trigger is, we need to intervene in the stress response. The first step is to be fully present. Breathe in deeply through the nose but don't get too focused on the breath in the early stages. For some people, focusing on the breath is not helpful. If this is the case for you, you need to save the breathwork for when you can practise it in a relaxed way and just breathe slowly and deeply through the nose. Alternatively, you can focus on the breath before an event or situation that you feel will be stressful or fear-inducing if you can do so calmly.

When in a situation of acute fear or panic, fully experience the feelings in your body. Do this with compassion and a sense of allowing rather than resisting. Be aware of where you have tense muscles, perhaps in the shoulders, consciously drop the shoulders, slacken the jaw, or relax whichever muscles have tensed up. Next, ground yourself. By this I mean sit or stand up tall. Feel your feet on the floor or ground. You could develop an automatic mantra of 'feel your feet'. By sticking to this simple script of 'feel your feet' the process is uncomplicated.

Trainers of airline pilots give them a script to learn to help them cope in a crisis. They learn a script so they don't have to react off the cuff. They know exactly what to say and do. By developing your own script to face a situation when your thinking brain has shut down and is being run by the limbic centre of the brain (the 'emotional' brain) you will know what to do without having to think about exactly what to do at that moment. This brief intervention gives a few seconds to gather your thoughts, to settle the distressing emotions and powerful hormones surging through the body. You can calm down and respond mindfully and rationally. Your brain will learn this new drill and you will be on the way towards some recovery from the tyranny of fear and panic. By sticking with the situation, you can rewire your brain's chemistry.

Avoidance will only feed the fear. By mindfully staying with the experience as best you can and seeing it through, fully aware, you are educating your brain to respond differently. You learn that you can feel fear, with all the physical sensations this brings, but that you will survive.

You can practise a sense of curious observation in your meditations, watching your thoughts and feelings without attaching emotion to them. This practice will help when you find yourself in a stressful situation. These sensations need not emotionally overwhelm you. They are just fleeting feelings. By sitting with the feelings, you learn that you can survive them. Practice being a detached observer.

Perhaps your stress or anxiety is of lower intensity. Perhaps you just have a vague sense of unease and find it hard to concentrate. Again, fully experience the feeling or sensation without judgment and with curious compassion for yourself rather than thinking: "Oh no, there I go again, messing up, making mistakes, and forgetting what I am supposed to be doing, what's wrong with me? Why I can't I just knuckle down and get on with it…" and so on.

Just observe your feelings and reactions. Stop berating yourself and acknowledge what is going on. For example, you could think to yourself: "I have found it hard to focus today. I wonder why that is? I see I am tense. Let's relax those muscles… let's take a few deep breaths… I will concentrate on what I am experiencing right now and just slow down…". You might feel that this is an indulgence you haven't got time for. Just be willing to try it. It will only take seconds. Also, consider the alternative: if your panic just builds, how productive or effective will you be?

To underline this point of taking a few seconds to experience your feelings and reactions, I will refer to a situation that is stressful by anyone's standards. In some medical schools in the U.S. when student doctors are being trained to deal with an acute medical emergency such as a patient who is suffering a heart attack, the students are told to take their own pulse first. By doing this, the students are getting feedback about their physiological state, and the few seconds it takes to feel the pulse gives them a moment to go into the situation with presence of mind.

When your mind feels scattered and panic builds, take a few seconds to experience the present moment as it feels for you, ground yourself, observe, breathe, and let go.

Approach all these activities with compassion and willingness. If you have made a plan and tried it out, adjust your plan if you need to. Just ease yourself a little out of your comfort zone each time. Err on the side of caution and easiness. Celebrate the next step accomplished. Share your plan and successes with a therapist, close friend, or family member. You need not do this alone.

You are not a victim in life. You do not have to be at the mercy of stressful feelings. You can cope in the short term and the long term if you approach your situation with awareness, compassion, and patience and take some positive action.

Elsewhere in the book, I talk about resourcing and non-resourcing activities. Resourcing activities are those that help soothe you, calm you, and help you reinvigorate, recuperate, or feel renewed. Use this as a benchmark for what you give your attention to. For you, which is more fulfilling and refreshing – a beach walk with a close friend and sharing a delicious lunch, or a day spent watching back-to-back movies? The answer is entirely up to you but give your attention to what *you* find resourcing. Life and time are precious, too precious to let drift by in aimless, reactive, and purposeless scrolling through screens, or spent in a half-here, half-there situation.

Take a few moments to consider what you find resourcing. Are there any common themes between the activities? Is there a balance between activities you carry out alone and with others? Do you enjoy being in nature or around animals? Make up your own bank of ideas to have to hand.

Whatever is on your list, make sure that is what you give your attention to. We all have activities we have to do every day (or face the consequences of not doing them). These are activities such as personal hygiene, cooking, eating, shopping for food, working and perhaps travelling to work or taking children to school. Try to undertake these duties and responsibilities as mindfully as you can. That means using your senses to tune into what is going on internally and in your environment. Bring your attention and the attitudes of mindfulness we have already discussed to these situations. Everyday tasks and activities can become more tolerable and even enjoyable.

Try to build in some resourcing activities such as journaling. You may have had a taste of this by now if you have kept a notebook in which to record your observations as you go through this book and its suggestions. A journal can be a handwritten record or a file on your computer. It is just for your personal use. You can write about anything you want. Just putting thoughts down on paper or a screen can help us process difficult emotions or make sense of a stressful event.

You can also chart progress or areas you want to focus on. In *The Artist's Way,* Julia Cameron recommends 'morning pages' [1]. This means writing down anything that comes to mind when you first wake up in the morning before you get caught up in the events and demands of the day. This can help clear the mind and free up our attention for the day ahead. You may prefer to write down a few thoughts before you go to sleep at night. There is no right or wrong way. Just do what works for you. Don't feel you have to keep a journal. If it doesn't work for you, try some supportive self-talk, or a video diary or letter writing. Experiment with what feels comfortable for you.

Movement can be refreshing and rejuvenating. Perhaps a leisurely walk through the park, or a ten-minute stretching sequence. Really experience the movement. Be aware of how your body and mind feel – don't just go through the motions – and have regular, mini movement breaks during the day. See the suggestions for mindful movement in the appendix.

If you enjoy cooking, immerse yourself in the process. Appreciate the vibrant colours of vegetables and fruits. Savour the aromas and taste of the food. If you are preparing the meal to share with a partner, friend, or family, think about how you are showing your love and care for them by preparing nutritious and delicious food. Play relaxing music in the background and enjoy the process.

By observing yourself and your feelings about your daily activities, you might notice an activity with which you get so absorbed that time seems to fly by. Note this. During this activity, did you have time to feel anxious or stressed? When you are clear about what activities you get absorbed in, build in more of them into your daily routine. This could be anything from practising yoga to doing a crossword, reading a novel, or building a website. These are activities meaningful to you. It doesn't matter if someone else thinks it is the most boring activity on earth, this is about what matters to you.

Make time for these activities. You might even consider pursuing the activity as a way of earning a living, particularly if your current occupation is causing you stress or anxiety. Just continue to observe and adjust as necessary. See your mindfulness practice as a sensitive navigation instrument that can continually give you feedback to help you develop confidence in yourself.

Notice what works for you and give these activities your time and attention. Some other resourcing activities to consider are listening to music or playing an instrument. Try music you don't normally listen to. I recently discovered Manouche jazz after being convinced all my life that I disliked jazz intensely. Read for pleasure: there is nothing like losing yourself in an enjoyable book. Read widely and voraciously. Enjoy curling up with a good book and relax. Sleep and rest: relaxation in the form of enjoying nature, listening to guided meditations, or visualisations. Meditation: this can be guided meditations or sitting quietly, observing your thoughts if you are comfortable doing this. You might enjoy listening to meditations on apps. Nature: walking, hiking, and sitting on a beach or in a forest are all restorative and relaxing activities. Laughter: Chatting with a friend or family member who helps us see the funny side of life. Watching a funny movie or episode of a comedy series helps us put things into perspective and not take life and ourselves so seriously.

When you are involved in an activity or spend time with a person, do so with attention to how you feel during and after the activity. Be aware of people or places that bring you down or stir up feelings of shame, anxiety, or worry. Think about how you could limit these activities to make space for those that help you feel uplifted, hopeful, and optimistic about life.

So, as this chapter draws to a close, consider how you use your attention. What do you focus on each day? How much attention do you give loved ones in your life? Is your attention constantly split between different things? Are you tempted to multi-task continuously? Do our drift into autopilot? Could you spend a few moments each morning setting an intention for the day to adopt a mindfulness attitude? Each day try to give yourself some time to enjoy an activity that you find resourcing and uplifting. If you need to make any changes regarding how you use your attention, do so with self-compassion.

Meditation 3: Attention.

In this meditation on attention, when I refer to the breath, just breathe well. That means breathing deeply into the lower abdomen and breathing slowly. If this is troublesome for you, just focus on the bodily sensations and let the breath just flow in and out naturally.

Please note that this meditation will focus on sounds in the room where you are. You will, therefore, need to listen on the speakers on your device, or if using earbuds, have just one earbud inserted and one ear free to pick up on the ambient sounds you can hear.

Settle into a comfortable position on a chair or mat. Gently close your eyes and bring attention to the body. Be aware of all the points of contact your body makes with the surface that is supporting your body. If you are on a chair, this could be your spine making contact with the back of the chair, the sensation of your feet on the floor, and the area around the buttocks as you sit on the chair.

If you are lying on a bed or mat be aware of the back of the head, the back, the backs of the thighs, calves and the backs of the heels as they make contact with and are supported by the surface you are lying on.

Other thoughts may come into your mind, this is normal and natural. Don't struggle with the thoughts, just let them go and bring your attention back to the body. Have a sense of looseness and heaviness in the body. Relax into this comfortable feeling but keep an alert awareness. Just notice how your body feels today. Be aware of any areas of tension or tightness.

Deepen the breath, breathing into the chest, feeling the ribcage expand. On the next in-breath, bring the breath right the way down into the abdomen. This will open the diaphragm, creating more space for the lungs. If other thoughts intrude, bring your attention back to the breath. Keep your attention focused on the sensations in the body and on the breath. Stay with this focus for a few moments, allowing other thoughts to drift off with the out-breath.

Now still with your eyes closed, bring your attention to any sounds in the room. Allow your ears to pick up on the smallest sound that you can perceive in the room. This could be the rustle of your clothes as you breathe in and out, the sound the air makes as it enters and leaves the nostrils, the hum from an electrical device, or the ticking of a clock.

Next, bring your attention to any noises you are aware of outside of the room or building you are in. This might be traffic, a dog barking, people's voices, or children playing. Pick out individual sounds and focus on one sound at a time, discriminating between sounds. Do this without judgement or any internal opinion on sound preferences or otherwise, just immerse yourself in that sound. Now, focus on all the external sounds as one body of sound. Now, transfer your awareness back to the sounds in the room.

Spend a few moments discerning individual sounds, focus on one sound at a time.... after a few moments of this experience all the sounds you are aware of in the room. If there is silence in the room, pay attention to the silence. Let any other thoughts go. Focus on your breath and your body as you sit or lie, and on the sounds or the silence in the room.

Appreciate any second of complete non-thinking or mental quiet you may have. Immerse yourself in the stillness, keeping the focus on the breath and the body. Relax in this stillness for a few moments...

After a few moments, deepen the breath. Recall a mental picture of the room you are in, notice as many details as you can. Just see what comes to mind. Now let the picture go. Open your eyes and scan your eyes around the room, taking in the colours, shapes, contours, and details of the room, the furniture, and objects in the room. Do this without judgement. Just notice. Now, bring your arms up above your head, breathe in, and enjoy a full body stretch. Pause for a second to be grateful for any moments of stillness or focused attention you experienced and carry on with your day with a spirit of calm but alert attention to what it brings.

Chapter Four: Attachment and Letting Go.

"Happiness is your nature. It is not wrong to desire it. What is wrong is seeking it outside when it is inside."
– Ramana Maharshi.

***

Louise and Vikki sat together on her sofa, shoulders touching as they looked at the large photograph album open on the coffee table in front of them. Vikki had always been the confident one. There were photos of Vikki on her bike, Vikki winning a race at sports day, Vikki trekking up Snowdonia for her Duke of Edinburgh Award. Louise felt the usual pang of inadequacy. In most of the photos, Louise was absent or pictured hiding behind her mum and dad. She was the shy, sensitive younger sister, protected by her dad who seemed all powerful back then, when she was five or six. Her mum had been wary of strangers and worried endlessly about safety. After their parents' fatal car crash, Vikki had pushed herself out into the world, relishing one challenge after another. Louise had retreated into her own world of books, drawing, and painting, feeling frightened and alone. Louise sighed deeply and wished so much she could be that little girl again with her mum and dad, safe and protected.

***

Rob stepped back and surveyed his work for the morning. He had filled two black bin bags with old clothes and shoes. He held his old work uniform in his hands as memories flooded back of the noisy car factory, the sounds of clashing metal, welding and drilling that dominated his life for thirty years. He had been good at his job and enjoyed the banter with his workmates and the predictable pattern of his days and weeks, filled with work, football, and trips to the pub with his pals. All that stopped when the factory closed. That's when he began to feel anxious about how to fill his time. The hours and days just ahead seemed blank and empty. He worried about paying bills and couldn't face his mates in the pub. He had gone a few times over the past few months but usually left early, as the noise, hustle and bustle of the jolly crowd sent him into a spin of panic so bad he thought he would pass out. Now he just stayed at home. With a sigh, he placed is old work clothes into the bin bag. He wasn't sure who he was anymore.

***

As humans, we are hard-wired to attach to places, people, and things. This is part of our survival mechanism. As babies, we need to attach to our caregivers to ensure we have all the essentials to survive and prosper. If young children do not have a consistent, loving caregiver in their early days and years, they suffer from attachment disorder, which can have huge implications for their later life.

As we mature, we need to make friends, form bonds with colleagues, neighbours, and friends. These attachments are all necessary for our emotional and mental health. Researchers such as Buettner have shown such bonds and support to help elongate a healthy life (see 'Blue Zones') [1]. These human interactions release feel-good hormones such as serotonin. Since the dawn of time, humans have needed to be together to ensure safety and survival. We thrive on these social connections and bonds.

The problem with attachment is that we suffer when we can't have what we have come to depend on for security, familiarity, or comfort. We suffer a sense of loss or lack, which can trigger profound sadness and depression. Fear of loss can trigger anxiety or even panic. So, as human beings, with all our hard wiring for attachments, how do we avoid the pitfalls?

This is a real human dilemma. We need attachments such as family, friends, routines, hobbies, homes, and possessions. There is nothing inherently wrong in enjoying the pleasures life has to offer. But we have all experienced losses. We know life is transient and things change. Change is the one constant in life. Sometimes we can initiate change, but often change is something that happens to us. We worry about losing our job, home, or family. Or we fear being put into a situation we think we cannot cope with, or that will cause us pain (aversion).

Attachments can become tricky for us if we hang on to them too tightly. Things change, time moves on, people grow and develop. We need room in our lives to let our attachments change, grow, and develop as our lives move forward. As fear of loss and change can be the cause of much anxiety and stress, we hang on to unhealthy habits or ways of responding, undermining physical and emotional health. Also, we might hold on to an unrealistic view of ourselves or onto a role that has passed.

Our brains love familiarity, so attaching to places, habits, or people is our brain's way of making sure we do nothing too rash and stick to known options. By doing what is familiar, we feel safe. Having our object of attachment removed or rearranged can generate feelings of anxiety and cause us to clutch more tightly to what we fear losing, whether this is an object, habit, or view of ourselves.

Attachments are a part of life and how we function as humans. Look at them as helpful barometers of our emotional health. The ferocity with which we hang on to an attachment can show where our values, expectations, and assumptions about life are. By feeling the discomfort or pain around challenges to our attachments, we can be more aware of ourselves. By practising this with compassion and gentleness, you can uncover much about how you function. When noticing attachments, do so without harsh judgment or criticism.

You might notice that you are attached to an idea or view of yourself or another person. In Rob's case, in the example at the beginning of this chapter, he was attached to the concept of himself as a working man and struggled to adapt to being unemployed. Rob's situation was imposed on him. However, you might want to make a change but feel anxious about taking action to initiate change, which can be very disconcerting. But letting the anxiety rule your life can stifle growth and change. For example, you might want to change jobs, change careers, or start a course of study, but fear is holding you back. Attachment to what feels safe and familiar is getting the upper hand even if you know rationally you will be in a better position if you make a change. Fear holds you back. If you find that anxiety about the change is stopping you from making positive change, try looking at the feeling as just an attachment to the familiar. So, experience the fear, thank it for taking care of you, and take one small step to initiate the change you want to make. You can take things as slowly as you need to. The more you do this, the easier it will become.

We can also be very strongly attached to our ideas and opinions. A casual scroll through Facebook shows just how attached to their opinions some people are. Reflect on a recent debate or argument you have had. How fiercely did you defend your corner? How firmly did you hang on to your side of the argument? Remember to reflect on these aspects of behaviour with a spirit of curiosity and compassion.

Think about the strength or intensity of your reactions and ask why. What could this show about what is going on for you? For example, I remember once some years ago we had a family get together. My then ten-year-old son was present. He was talking animatedly to his uncle about television adverts. In a joking sort of way, his uncle commented on how much television my son must watch. I immediately felt a rush of anger and upset. *How dare he say my son watches too much television – he doesn't! Is he trying to insinuate I am a neglectful mother?* I think you probably get the picture. I said nothing. I appeared to ignore the comment, and the conversation turned to something else.

However, when I took a few minutes to calm down, I thought about my reaction with a sense of compassion and curiosity. Was there any truth in this? Why did I react (albeit internally) so defensively? I realized I was attached to the ideal of myself as a good mother, and that ideal was being challenged. I knew that I had been extremely busy in the time leading up to this Christmas family gathering. I worked full-time in a demanding job and had a home to run and a family to take care of. Perhaps my son did watch a lot of television as I bustled about cleaning, cooking, and trying to keep on top of the demands of my job, which often involved work at home. This led me to think about how I might get some help with taking care of the house. Perhaps I could get a cleaner for a few hours a week. Maybe I could relax my standards a bit. I could make simpler meals and get shopping delivered.

I talked to my son about activities he might like to do outdoors. We planned a camping trip. He joined a football club. We went for more walks along the beach and in the countryside. We spent some time on craft projects at home. My relative's comments, which I found painful and could have resulted in a big family bust-up, were a helpful wake-up call. I could have had a fight with my relative or chastised myself, heaping on the shame and guilt. I could have felt like a victim. Poor me, with all this work to do while he is just having a go at me. However, with a spirit of curiosity and compassion, the comment was the catalyst for a positive change to our routine. Looking back, I could thank my relative for this comment. The changes we made meant that we created lots of happy memories, doing lovely things that we would have missed out on if we had carried on mindlessly in the usual way.

It can be painful to look at ourselves objectively or re-evaluate our behaviour in response to valid feedback or constructive criticism. However, being overly attached to a certain view of ourselves and being unable to accept reasonable criticism can stifle growth and change. Let's go back to Max to help shed light on this point:

Max hated going anywhere near his staff room at work. He stomped up the stairs towards the door of the staffroom. He could hear some of his colleagues talking over their coffee. With horror, he realized they were talking about him. They used words such as 'grumpy git' and cited examples of how rude he could be with customers. Max slunk off to the men's toilets. It crushed him to hear this criticism. How dare they? Who do they think they are, anyway? He slammed the door of the toilets and decided he would speak to his manager and go home sick.

Max's problems with his colleagues have built up over time. He has consistently avoided considering how he comes across to others. His aversion to looking at his reactions has compounded his issues with the other staff members.

By 'allowing' Max could accept that the criticism is valid and do something about it. Perhaps he has been grumpy. Perhaps he has been rude to customers. He could register the uncomfortable feelings that such criticism can raise. He could consider why such criticism evokes such overwhelming reactions in him. Why is he so disturbed by other people's evaluations of his behaviour?

With an attitude of allowing, Max can learn more about himself and find solutions to the issues he has at work. By resisting and reacting with anger, Max moves away from a solution, compounds the problems with his colleagues, and rather than starting to let go of what is not resourcing him (self-doubt, angry responses, emotional pain) Max holds onto it grimly, nursing his resentments about his work colleagues.

***

In his book *The Pleasure Trap,* Dr Doug Lisle explains how as humans we are programmed to seek pleasure and avoid pain [2]. This makes sense when we consider our choices in food, home comforts, and habits. It seems natural to enjoy foods that are satisfying and tasty. We like being warm and cosy, so we crank up the central heating. We avoid situations that make us feel physically or emotionally uncomfortable. We get attached to our comfortable habits and routines.

This makes us feel safe and secure. Why not seek pleasure and avoid pain? It seems a natural and common-sense thing to do. Why would anyone seek anything else? Who wants pain in their life?

Perhaps your fear of *any* pain or discomfort – a natural response – has become exaggerated. Any minor threat you perceive to your comfort or security signals a red alert, triggering anxious thoughts. By seeing your disturbance as a natural (although not necessarily a rational response) to a minor infringement of your physical, emotional, or mental comfort and attachment to pleasure, you can put your anxiety into perspective.

It's simply attachment to a certain state or feeling. Just because your boss looked at you with what you thought was a disapproving look doesn't mean you have to go into full-scale panic. It's just an attachment to the pleasant feelings of security and acceptance you get when your boss smiles at you. By being aware of our reactions, we can get some insight into our emotions we have when our attachments feel threatened, and some control over how we respond. Being aware of intense attachments can also help us figure out what triggers our anxiety or fear.

It is useful to consider your attachments for many reasons. It helps highlight areas of sensitivity in your life. Perhaps you get touchy if anyone criticizes your work. Why is this? Asking these sorts of questions can help uncover many aspects of your character and conditioning.

Consider for a few moments what you count as your pleasures in life. Maybe write them down in your journal. It doesn't matter what they are. This is just for you. No one will come along to judge. Now write down what causes you pain – whatever comes to mind. This is information for you.

As you reflect on what gives you pleasure and what causes you pain, rate your level of attachment to the things you feel give you pleasure or that you are strongly attached to. Perhaps rate them on a scale of 1 to 10. 1 being little to 10 being massively attached to something. Consider which attachments or pleasures that serve you in terms of health and well-being, emotional and mental. These could form the basis of your self-care plan. Now, look at the attachments that don't serve you. Do they ultimately hurt you and provoke anxiety, worry, negative thinking, unjust criticism, or a mind-set of scarcity? Perhaps you are overly attached to a version of yourself from the past, maybe a job or family role that you no longer have? Perhaps you are deeply fearful of losing a role you currently have in life?

Later this chapter, we will look at how to let go of these attachments that don't serve you. What serves us at one stage in our life might not in another season of life. We constantly need to re-evaluate and let go. A mindfulness practice can help us regularly re-evaluate our lives, intentions, attachments, and goals. Like a snake shedding its skin, we need to grow, develop, and move on, letting go of what we no longer need.

Let's look at another real-life example:

Gerry enjoyed going to the pub for a few drinks. He felt buoyed up by the buzz from the alcohol. When his doctor told him to cut back on his drinking, he suddenly felt a bolt of panic about seeing his mates at the pub without a drink. He couldn't do it. Whenever he thought of any social occasion, he always associated it with alcohol. He couldn't face people in a social situation without a drink in his hand.

In terms of attachment and aversion, Gerry saw that he was over attached to alcohol and he had a fear of appearing boring or tongue-tied in company. He felt that the drink gave him the courage he needed to face people. Digging deeper and examining his anxiety around social situations gave Gerry insight into how and why he had been using alcohol as a crutch. This reflection opened up areas that Gerry had never considered before. He realized that if he tackled his social anxiety and his feelings of inadequacy, he could let go more easily of his attachment to having an alcoholic drink in his hand at every social event or function.

(Powerful attachments to substances such as alcohol, drugs, or food fall into the category of addictions and are beyond the scope of this book. If you or someone close to you needs guidance about alcohol use, I recommend *Alcohol And You* and *The 10-Day Alcohol Detox Plan,* both by addictions therapist Lewis David and which, like my books, are available from WinsPress.com.)

These deep attachments referred to as addictions are not just confined to substances such as alcohol or drugs. Shopping, hoarding, electronic devices, gambling, sex, porn, and food are all subjects of addiction. These types of attachments will cause serious problems in terms of relationships, self-esteem, health, finances, and work performance.

Over the next day or so, just notice when you feel a sense of loss, or fear of loss, or a compulsion to do something. Look at your behaviour objectively, with compassion for yourself and curiosity about your feelings. Make a note in your journal of what you notice. Describe your feelings around these observations and ensure you avoid any self-criticism. You are making an inventory of what you see. You need not analyse it or make any attempt at changing it at this point. Just notice what you see with a spirit of enquiry and gentle interest. An example of the sort of behaviour might be noticing how times a day you pick up your phone and scroll it with no purpose. Look at this with curiosity: how often do you do this in company, or when you are with your children or partner?

Think about the last time you looked at Facebook. Where were you, what else were you doing, who were you with, why did you want to look at Facebook, what was your motivation? Next time you look at Facebook, or other favourite social media, consider these questions and just notice your reactions to what you see on the site. Perhaps you go through an entire range of emotions: pleasure if someone likes a comment you have posted, irritation at unflattering comments, and perhaps a stab of jealousy when you see photos of a friend on an amazing holiday. You were perhaps feeling calm and happy when you picked up your phone, but within seconds of looking at the social media site, you felt disgruntled and dissatisfied with your life.

These bursts of discontent or dissatisfaction erode our joy in life. Deeper feelings of resentment or anxiety can creep in. If we are already feeling low or vulnerable, seeing a multitude of photos that appear to show how happy, successful, and healthy so many other people look can leave us feeling like the odd one out.

There is nothing wrong with social media per se. It's a brilliant way to keep in touch with family, friends, and acquaintances. Joining groups can be a fantastic source of support or a way of getting involved in your local community. The problem is when we feel the urge to check is multiple times an hour and end up feeling dissatisfied with our life.

So, over the next few days, when you feel a compulsion to do something or you are aware of an attachment to people, places, or things, ask yourself some questions. Does the attachment serve you? Is it healthy? How does it impact on feelings of anxiety or stress? How would you feel if it were no longer present in your life? Is it time to let it go? Are you aware of any aversion to letting it go? If you want to let something go, perhaps a damaging habit, do you need to get some help to do so?

***

In the Buddhist tradition, there is a monthly ritual of visiting the charnel ground, a kind of cemetery. They do this to reflect on the transience of life and the reality of things constantly changing. I appreciate that if you are already feeling low, this might be the last thing you feel like thinking about. But bear with me. Considering these aspects of life gives balance. Today in the West, we don't want to consider change, loss, or having to let go. We are so focused on acquiring or developing what we have. We see loss as negative.

This underlying fear of loss can cause a sense of free-floating anxiety. For most of us, the fear of losing people, places, or things near and dear to us can cause genuine pain. How then can we let go of this pain?

If holding on tightly to attachments is causing us pain, then letting go is the doorway to freedom. To illustrate this, I will refer to an old Asian fable about a greedy monkey. Traditionally monkey traps were made from coconut shells. An empty coconut shell would contain a banana. A gap would be cut into the shell that was just big enough for the monkey to get his hand in to grab the banana. However, the gap was fashioned in such a way as to make it impossible for the monkey to get his hand out with the banana. If he let go of the banana, he could remove his hand and be free. This analogy illustrates how many of us can be trapped by our desires, habits, attachments, and wants. If we let go, we can be free.

We might need to let go of strategies we have developed to cope with the demands of life. We might need to let go of worry, rumination, rushing, unrealistically lofty standards, and perfectionism; or unhealthy habits such as smoking, people-pleasing, and criticising ourselves. By letting go of such behaviours, we make space for more nourishing ways of coping with life. Take a moment now to reflect on any habits you need to let go of – habits that might be contributing to feelings of anxiety.

The shortfall between our expectations and reality can cause a lot of angst and worry. Have you ever woken up on a special day such as Christmas Day or a birthday and had certain expectations of how that day would be? Perhaps you put in a lot of effort with preparations in the kitchen or organizing an enormous party. You run through your mind about how you think the day or special event will go. After all the effort and hard work, you expect the day to be simply perfect. Often, this is not what happens. Life has a funny way of throwing a spanner in the works. Things can turn out differently from what we expected. That initial hope and elation can be dashed as the reality cannot match up to our expectations. You worry that it won't be perfect and beat yourself up because you 'failed'. So, let go of expectations and accept how things turn out. Worry and self-reproach won't make things any better.

Perhaps you have been on holiday to a beautiful place out of season. It is quiet and you have the luxury of walking on empty beaches and always being able to get 'your' seat at your favourite restaurant. The grounds around the hotel are quiet and you can always get 'your' sunbed by the pool. However, you go back in July and you feel quite put out by all the crowds. You feel mildly upset that the friendly waiter at your favourite restaurant hasn't kept 'your' table by the window for you, and he hardly seems to remember you. You can't find any free sunbeds, and the beach is so crammed by sunbathers, you have to pick your way through them on your walk. It's all very disconcerting. You feel perhaps that the holiday has been spoiled as this place is not as you remembered it. You were attached to your idea or expectation of what this place is like. The mismatch between your expectation and reality has caused the disappointment.

Sometimes we expect a lot from other people. We expect them to match up to our high ideals of honesty or good cheer. If we then discover a small indiscretion, we feel betrayed. Perhaps your partner is usually cheerful but has an off day and you feel devastated. You might even conclude that they are off because of something you have done or said, when they are just in poor form because of feeling unwell physically – it has nothing to do with you.

You might even have high expectations of people or expect them to know what you need or would like without even communicating this to them. Because the other person is unaware of your expectations, they cannot live up to them, and you feel let down. This happens with couples all the time. It can cause unnecessary friction and negative emotions all round.

As human beings, we like to visualize how we would like things to turn out. However, emotionally we can come unstuck when we get overly attached to the outcomes, especially when the plan involves unpredictable variables such as other people. The problem with other people is that they just don't do what we always expect them to do! By letting go of fixed ideas about outcomes, we are 'allowing'. This means we are allowing space for whatever is going on.

Traits such as perfectionism can eat away at your motivation and self-esteem. If you feel everything needs to be done perfectly, you will feel constantly worried. Let go of perfectionism. Good enough is good enough. Replace perfectionism with a growth mind-set. Remind yourself that it is okay to mess up. You are human. You will make mistakes. Share your mistakes, laugh at them, and see how they have helped you to learn and grow.

Be compassionate with yourself. Let go of self-punishment and shame. Give yourself credit for the gains you have made. Don't beat yourself up. Punishment and shame never work as a lasting motivator. Let go of the stick and reward yourself with the carrot. Let go of criticising. Allow compassion and curiosity to soften judgements about yourself and other people.

Let go of all-or-nothing or black-and-white thinking. People are not all good or all bad. A rainy day is not just bad. A meal you have cooked that didn't turn out as expected is not necessarily bad. You are not a good spouse or a bad spouse. Most days are not all good or all bad. Life has a range of shades and nuances. Most of it is coloured by our perceptions, attitudes, and beliefs.

Let go of the need to be always right. Accept that your perception of a situation, problem, or issue might not be correct. There might be another way of looking at it. Keep an open mind. Be willing to see situations from the point of view of others. Allow things to happen. Let life unfold. Let go of striving. This can be difficult, especially for our western mind-set. For now, try not to force anything.

Let go of fear of lack. Enough is good enough. Give yourself to life. Enjoy the agreeable feelings that come from being generous and thoughtful of others. With a compassionate attitude, look at your fears or anxiety around material loss or financial insecurity. Remind yourself regularly of what you have. Practice gratitude for what you have.

Let go of catastrophizing and watch your language. How often do you use overdramatic words such as awful, terrible, shocking, and horrible? Be mindful of how you think about events in your life and how you express yourself to others. Using overly dramatic language can contribute to the feeling that your life is unsafe and frightening.

Take a moment now to reflect on what you need to let go of. Just pick out one or two things and work on those to begin with. Pick something easy for you and celebrate your success, then move onto something more difficult. If there is something that you baulk at, cultivate a sense of willingness. Remember to take small, steady steps, and keep it simple.

By now you may have thought of a habit, attitude, or attachment you would like to let go of, but how do you let go? The following are some practical ideas.

Firstly, simply focus on the breath. Be aware of letting go of stale air and the need to take in fresh air. As you breath consciously, set the intention to let go of anything that does not serve you.

Visualization is a powerful tool in letting go. Don't worry if you feel you do not have a good visual imagination. You can use the senses that work best for you in an imaginative situation. For example, if sound works for you, you could imagine having a conversation with someone about moving on or changing in some way. You can also use everyday experiences to imagine you are letting go, such as washing away anything that is not needed in the shower, bath, or when washing hands.

I have mentioned journaling as a method to pour out intense feelings or thoughts. Spending time letting it all spill out onto paper means you can let go of troublesome thoughts that go around endlessly in your mind. If you are worried about someone else finding your writing, you could safely burn the paper or destroy it, which can add to the powerful sense of letting it go. You could write a letter to say goodbye to someone or explain how you are letting them go. You do not need to necessarily send the letter.

Movement can be a method to let go of overwhelming feelings such as anger or resentment. You are feeling the emotions and not resisting them, but you are letting the emotion move through you so you can let go of it in a healthy way.

You can take practical actions such as opening windows or letting go of objects that have painful memories or drag you back to the past. As an act of self-care, you could look around your home for items such as artwork, photos, or decorative pieces that have any negative memories or emotions attached to them and let them go.

You can use your imagination to let go in whatever way is helpful to you. The simplest and most gently effective way to let go of fear or overwhelm is to just sit quietly with the intention. Put your hand on your heart, slow the breath and, as you breath out, do so with the intention of letting go of what is troubling you.

The guided meditation coming up next can also be used as a support in the process of letting go of any attachments, troubling feelings, or memories. Use it an often as you need to.

Meditation 4: Attachment.

Sit in a position comfortable for you, either upright in a chair, cross-legged on a cushion on the floor or lying on a bed or mat. However, you sit or lie, ensure that you can hold that position comfortably for about five minutes. If you need to adjust your position, please do so.

To begin, focus your attention on how your body touches the surface you are sitting or lying on. Be aware of where your body is in contact with the surface. Be aware of areas that feel softer or harder than others. Bring your attention to any areas that might feel stiff or tense. Breathe in deeply and focus on the breath. As you breathe out, breathe a sense of warmth and relaxation to the parts of the body that feel tight. With each exhalation, relax the body. Allow the body to become still and calm.

Just note any sensations in the body.

Bring your attention back to the breath. Allow for a sense of expansion and awareness. Allow yourself to enjoy these few moments of peace.

As you sit in the present moment, allow yourself to experience all that is you. Have a relaxed, calm awareness of all aspects of what makes you: your judgements, your worries, your experiences, your attachments. See them all with a compassionate attitude. Bring softness to your awareness. Keep your focus on the breath and on noticing all that makes you who you are in the present moment. Breath in peace and calm, breathe out peace and calm.

Connect with a deep part of yourself. See yourself as you are right now. Look at your concerns, worries, and attachments with a gentle curiosity. Accept how you are. See all that you feel is good and all that you feel is bad with equanimity and calmness. Be aware of any potent feelings that might come up and breathe into them – breathing in and breathing out, accepting where you are. Let the breath act as a balm on any disturbance or harsh self-judgment that might arise.

Focus on a sense of infinite space and openness inside your being that has room for all that you are. As you breathe in, smile; as you breathe out, let go of all that does not serve you. Spend a few moments focusing on a gentle smile as you breathe in and letting go of all that is unneeded in your life. That could be attachments, turbulent feelings, resentments, worries, or assumptions.

Know that you are learning how to let go with love and acceptance of where you are now. Sit easily knowing that any letting go is a gentle process. Be accepting of yourself as you are now. You need not strive or struggle. Allow this feeling of complete self-acceptance to permeate your whole being.

Now, as you breathe out, have a sense of this complete acceptance radiating out to the others in the room, the building, the town, the country, and on out to an acceptance of all people just as they are. For a few moments focus on a sense of compassionate understanding for all living things, their struggles, their challenges, joys, and woes, all with a calm acceptance of the here and now.

Now bring your awareness back to your body. Focus on the sounds you can hear in the room or just outside of the room. In your mind's eye, picture the room you are in. Now open your eyes and bring yourself back to the here and now. Smile, stretch gently, and continue with your day.

Chapter Five: Finding Peace and Happiness

"Each step along the Buddha's path to happiness requires practising mindfulness until it becomes part of your daily life." – Henepola Gunaratana.

***

Louise looked anxiously at the clock. She couldn't believe that it was 8.45 a.m. already. She felt a fleeting palpitation in her chest as she rushed around her flat, gathering up her packed lunch, phone, and handbag. The previous evening, Louise had stayed up, engrossed in a TV drama. She felt tired and stressed as she threw on her coat and locked the door. She would be late for work – again. Louise ran out of her building and towards the bus stop, her phone clutched to her ear, ringing work to apologise. The bus went past her at speed, splashing her as it drove through a deep puddle. Louise stood, wet and out of breath, feeling like life was all just too much.

***

It was ages since Rob had visited his local park. He had been holed up in that flat all winter. He sat down on a bench and felt the gentle, spring sunshine on his face. He had just been to see his mum. He had decided to walk back home through the park and felt lulled by the rhythm of his walk, the warmth of the sunshine, and the sounds of children playing. He tuned into the sounds, closing his eyes for a few seconds. He became aware of the birds chirruping happily and a distant hum of traffic.

The pleasant ordinariness of the situation helped settle his nerves, jangled from the latest mini drama concerning his mum. He deliberately slowed down his breathing as he reflected on the morning. He had arrived at his mum's house earlier, the steps by her front door littered with the remains of a smashed bottle of tomato sauce. Hearing her wail inconsolably about how the bottle had dropped out of her shopping bag and smashed on the steps made his stomach lurch with pity, worry and frustration. He had spent the morning helping her clear up and answering her repeated questions about shopping and medical appointments.

As Rob sat on the park bench, breathing slowly, and looking around him, a welcome wave of peace washed over him. Rob reminded himself that right now, he was okay.

***

This being human is a guest house.

Every morning a new arrival.

A joy, a depression, a meanness,

some momentary awareness comes,

as an unexpected visitor.

Welcome and entertain them all!

Even if they are a crowd of sorrows,

who violently sweep your house,

empty of its furniture,

still, treat each guest honourably.

He may be clearing you out

for some new delight.

The dark thought, the shame, the malice.

meet them at the door laughing and invite them in.

Be grateful for whatever comes.

because each has been sent,

as a guide from beyond.

– Rumi

***

Understandably, most of us want to feel happy most of the time. However, can we really chase happiness? Happiness itself has shades of meaning and nuances of feeling: content, cheerful, happy, excited, ecstatic, and so on. As the poem above states so eloquently, we will experience a range of emotions in any one day. We can't force any one emotion, such as feeling happy, but we can feel contended most of the time and not be assailed by powerful feelings of overwhelm or panic.

Most of us can be happy most of the time if we understand that feelings of contentment come as a by-product or side-effect of our choices, attention, behaviour, focus, biology, circumstances, and perspective. Some of these things we have control over; some of them we don't. By focusing on what we can control and optimising our choices, behaviour, and perceptions, we give ourselves the chance to feel calm and centred. This is not about forcing a particular feeling or even about positive thinking, but it is about treating ourselves compassionately and allowing for good feelings as well as accepting the less comfortable feelings. This gentle acceptance can lessen the stress created by resistance or struggle.

To maximise your chances of a serene, joyful life, you firstly need to be present in your life to work out what helps, what harms, and what you have some control over.

Sometimes we just need to accept our feelings as they are, just for today. Feelings are not facts. We can acknowledge them, but we don't have to be overwhelmed by them. We can feel angry and 'off', but we need not act out. Think about what you can do to feel more comfortable in a healthy, resourcing way. Take some action if you can and accept your feelings for now. They will pass.

As human beings, we will experience an entire spectrum of emotions. We can observe these with compassionate detachment. This does not mean shutting your feelings off. It just means not getting caught up in them, and not catastrophizing, blaming, or judging ourselves or other people. Just accept the feelings as part of the human condition.

An example that most women can probably relate to is the intense emotions around PMT. These feelings are genuine. You might get tearful or feel tense and on edge. If you can accept the feelings, understand it's just that time of the month, do your best to take care of yourself, and perhaps explain to close loved ones how you feel. You need not act out. Nor do you need to divorce your husband, move to a new house, or change jobs! It's just a feeling and it will pass. Acceptance and compassionate detachment can help us keep a calm head in the middle of intensely emotional experiences.

Sometimes emotional change can be seasonal. I know that in early January, I will hit a road bump of feeling low. I don't worry about this anymore. I accept how I feel and know it will pass. I try to appreciate the beauty of nature in wintertime and look for early signs of spring.

We can apply this to feelings of stress and anxiety. Accept your feelings, do what you can do to cope in healthy, resourcing ways, and don't overly attach to bodily sensations or powerful emotions. Accept them as something that will come and go.

If you are perturbed by distressing feelings associated with anxiety or stress, try this visualisation technique: Imagine you are on a beach in stormy weather. You see waves crashing onto the beach. You watch the waves arrive dramatically and then pull out slowly, some vast waves, some gentler waves. Breathe slowly and gently as you do this. See the waves as your feelings, gradually subsiding and becoming calm. You are not pushing back against how you feel or denying your feelings but techniques such as this visualization help to objectify the feelings and give you a few minutes to compose yourself.

By making healthy, enriching choices, we can enjoy the more joyful feelings that follow rather than endlessly chasing elusive happiness. We can be grateful and make choices that optimize more positive feelings. We can make space for the full spectrum of emotions that add to the richness of our human experience.

We all have stressors to deal with as we go out into the world, such as traffic, impatient people, hustle and bustle, sensory overload, unhelpful office or shop staff, and moody work colleagues. Sometimes the stressors might start even before we get out of bed: physical pain, crying babies, sick children, a toddler's wet bed. There is no getting away from it. Life is stressful. However, if we can use mindfulness techniques, we will be better able to cope with these stressors.

A study of senior medical students showed how a mindfulness practice reduced levels of stress and anxiety in students.[1] The students still had the same stresses – namely, long, exhausting shifts, exams, being observed by senior colleagues, and dealing with a myriad of patients' problems. However, with a mindfulness practice, their sense of calm, well-being, and the quality of the responsiveness and accuracy of their decisions on the ward all improved.

Life is full of challenges, issues, and problems. It is unreasonable and probably unwise to wish we had zero challenges in our lives. Problems and challenges are essential in developing maturity and wisdom. True creativity has problem-solving at its centre. Think how boring life would be with no challenges at all. Take on some challenges if you can. Try to welcome challenges as an aspect of life that makes it interesting and varied. By actively accepting challenges you are less likely to feel victimized by difficulties. Overcoming challenges will build resilience and self-confidence.

In managing stress, you can make some changes to help reduce it as best you can. You can incorporate a steady mindfulness practice into your day-to-day life. You can build up a toolbox of simple strategies and techniques to help stay calm and free from unnecessary anxiety. By approaching daily stressors with attitudes of mindfulness – such as a commitment to being present, acceptance, and compassion for ourselves and others – you will establish a stable base of calm and peace.

Modern life is full of micro-doses of stress throughout the day. We could view stressful sensations as 'terrible', shocking',' life-threatening', or 'panic-inducing' – or just view them calmly as perfectly normal physiological responses to stimuli. If you sense your heart beating rapidly or your breathing becoming fast and shallow, pause and take a moment to slow your breathing and accept that these responses are normal and natural in a situation in which we perceive threat. But there is no need to panic about the feelings themselves.

By regularly undertaking practices such as guided meditation, a body scan, or mindfulness movement activities, we are re-educating our nervous system and brain chemistry to recalibrate. Activities such as these will help you function from a calm base. If we are functioning from a peaceful core, minor potentially stressful stimuli will not have the dramatic effect they might do if we are already feeling frazzled and on edge.

Consistency is key. Have an intentional plan for activities such as listening to a guided meditation, not just a vague aspiration to do them when you can. Note down when you will listen to a meditation, read this book, or write in your journal. Schedule these activities into your calendar. If you have slipped back, re-commit to doing these short activities. The rewards you experience will be worth it. If it means getting up five minutes earlier in the morning, then set your alarm five minutes earlier. If it means switching off the television or Netflix five minutes earlier in the evening, then do that. If you consistently practise these techniques, you will feel calmer with minor time investment. Even just deciding to view yourself with more compassion will help.

In reducing anxiety and dealing with stressful feelings, you can take practical steps in your life to help you feel calmer. The following are some to consider: Be conscious and mindful of what you are eating and drinking regularly. Sugar, caffeine, and alcohol can all mimic the sensations of stress and anxiety. Caffeine and alcohol can also affect your quality of sleep. For most people, drinking a couple of cups of coffee before noon is a good rule to adhere to, and if you like an alcoholic drink in the evening, avoid drinking close to bedtime. Perhaps avoid habitually drinking every evening and find other ways to relax. Avoid sweets or high-sugar foods for your general health and weight. Eating too many sweet treats can give us a sugar rush that feels very much like the physiological stress response. Cutting down on sugar is an excellent move when seeking a calmer state.

Being more aware and mindful of the content you view on-screen or the material you read are all worth thinking about too. Binge-watching horror movies or sitting up to midnight reading psychological thrillers will not help you feel calm or sleep well. I know I have tried it!

Be aware of the noise levels in your home. Is there always a constant stream of noise from television sets or radios? Be more intentional with what you listen to and remember that a quiet environment can be very soothing. Just being aware of minute noises, birds singing, the hum of traffic and the wind in the trees can all help anchor you to the present.

Notice, how often you have the urge to check the news or social media. How regularly do you do it? At what time?

Where are you? Do you know why you have the urge to check the news or social media feed at any particular time? The object is not to tell yourself off, but to be aware of how you take in the news and what effect it is having on your emotional and mental health. Note down any observations in your journal.

Be aware of how you are responding to the people you encounter today. Even people you think you like. How do you feel after you have been with them? Do you feel tired or uplifted and optimistic? Notice your levels of stress or anxiety around the people you meet today.

When we experience the stress response, our physiological state is getting ramped up to move. So much of the detrimental effects of stress are because we are being primed to move, but we can't – for example, when we have just been cut up in the car at a roundabout, but we are restricted to our car seat. Stress hormones are rushing through your body, preparing you for a physical response, but you can't act on it. Any movement can help shake off the build-up of anxiety in the body. You might feel you need to get out for a run or a brisk walk to work through pent up stress from the day. Undoubtedly, rigorous exercise can help but don't feel that you always have to throw yourself full throttle into an intense exercise regime. Slow and gentle movement routines such as yoga or tai chi help soothe the nervous system and work deeply into muscles, joints, and areas of the body that have accumulated stress.

Whatever you do, do it mindfully. Pay attention to the breath and really experience how each movement feels. Try to keep your attention on what you are doing and the sensations you are experiencing. This will keep you calmer, more focused, and help to avoid injuries or damage as you will think about what you are doing rather than just throwing your body into it. If you have got into the routine of going to a busy gym with harsh lights, blaring music, and a pumped-up atmosphere, perhaps try something calmer like a run through a park or area of natural beauty. If you exercise regularly, consider how you do it. Do you run with no enjoyment on a treadmill in a busy gym with loud music? Plan in movement that you enjoy and feels good.

In this chapter, we have looked at some practical things you can do to help you feel calmer and less stressed. Having a personal inventory of your lifestyle – including eating, drinking, entertainment, and media exposure – can be a rewarding mindfulness exercise. Just take a few minutes to think about your daily habits and amend one aspect at a time. Perhaps make some notes in your journal.

***

In chapter two, we looked at how counterproductive multi-tasking is. Studies have shown that multi-taskers are in fact task-switchers who are less efficient and productive than their colleagues who mono-task. We saw how multi-tasking can bring on feelings of stress and anxiety because we are burdening the brain with a stressful experience.

Time can present challenges for those of us who feel stressed or anxious. There can be too much time and we feel it stretches ahead in huge blanks of nothingness. Or it can feel like there is too little time and we constantly feel harassed and behind on our schedules, and it can be tempting to multi-task to get more done in a shorter period of time.

When we accept that really the only time we have is now, we can think more helpfully about time. We can't be in tomorrow and we can't travel back to yesterday. By focusing on now, we bring our attention, emotions, feelings, and experiences right to this moment. When we are totally focused on this moment, we can be most productive and experience life to the full.

When we feel overwhelmed, we can chunk time for all the tasks we have to complete, without the temptation to multi-task and end up feeling more frazzled. By setting aside sufficient time to focus on one task, we know we can complete it well because we are giving it our full attention and effort. Chunking the day into slots for tasks, jobs, and more pleasurable activities – such as time with loved ones or a walk – we can use our time well and give the activity or person our full attention. If you use this chunking technique to allocate time for particular tasks or activities, allow for more time than you think you will need. As much as possible, be flexible with times. For example, don't commit yourself too tightly to a strict timetable. Keep times a bit loose to allow for any delays.

Try using your planner, diary, or calendar to block out chunks of time for the things you want to achieve or enjoy. Commit to them and give them your full attention. You will feel calmer, more satisfied, and achieve more.

The beauty of mindfulness is that so much of it is less to do with taking action than changing our attitudes, such as incorporating attitudes of mindfulness into our daily lives. Bring these attitudes to all your activities and interactions: compassion, acceptance, gratitude, patience, letting go, non-judging, non-striving, trust, and willingness. Just begin by focusing on a couple by setting an intention each day to be more compassionate or grateful in all your interactions. Keep practising and it will become second nature.

Kolb's learning theory gives a model of how we learn a new skill, whether that is learning how to use mindfulness in our lives or how to drive a car. There are four stages:

Stage one is when we are *unconsciously incompetent*. We don't know how to do something, and we are ignorant of the fact that we don't know how to do it. Before learning about mindfulness, I had no idea that I didn't know about these techniques and how beneficial they could be because I had not been exposed to the potential of the practices.

Stage two is when we are *consciously incompetent*. When I started to learn about mindfulness, I realized how much I didn't know, and I had to make an effort to learn about the techniques and apply them to my life. You will need to exert some effort to learn and apply the techniques and reflect on how you can develop the attitudes of mindfulness discussed.

Stage three is *conscious competence*. When we have learned the techniques and attitudes. We know what they are and what we need to do but must remember to do them or consciously bring them to mind to apply them.

Stage four is *unconscious competence*. This is the point we can get to when the techniques are embedded in our daily routines and we respond to the events of daily life with the mindfulness attitudes presented here. The benefit of this is that our mode of operating in the world, our relationships, reactions, and habits will become more guided by mindfulness principles and attitudes. They will become a natural part of who we are and how we move through our days. It does not mean we are unconscious – quite the opposite – but it does mean we can practice mindfulness more easily based on our developing experience and skill.

I refer to this theory because I want to highlight that we cannot just drift from stage one to stage four without some effort, practice, and mistakes. Expect to forget or to have days when you find it harder to react to a situation with the attitude you aspire to develop. As the expression goes: 'Easy does it – but do it!'

Consciously recall one or two of the mindfulness attitudes, such as compassion, patience, letting go, non-striving, gratitude, acceptance, non-judging, and willingness. Bring the attitudes to mind with everything you do today, from driving to work, waiting in line for your coffee, how you react to a critical email at work, or how you go about shopping for groceries in the evening. Bring compassion and curiosity to everything you do today and just see what you discover. If you forget, just gently bring your focus back. Make a note in your journal of anything that really strikes you.

When considering the impact of consciously applying mindfulness attitudes to your daily life, note how you feel when you do so. For example, if you are focusing on compassion and you are in line at the grocery store, how different does it feel if you wait with compassion while the elderly lady in front of you searches for small change? Do you feel calmer? Do you feel less stressed? If you do, make a note of this. The beneficial feelings you experience will help embed this behaviour in the reward centres of the brain. This means, with time and practice, your default reaction will be to respond with compassion rather than feel irritated, resentful, and ultimately stressed and harassed.

Bring the mindfulness attitudes we have talked about to as many of your daily routines as you can.

***

When we feel anxious or panicky about a situation, it is often because we feel we have no control. We might feel we need to control everything, but then feel overwhelmed by the enormous responsibility of everything we need to do. Let's be clear: we have some control over some things in life, but we don't have control over everything. In managing anxiety, we need to be honest with ourselves about what we can control and then make a plan.

By being curious and compassionate with yourself as you have worked through the preceding chapters, you have practised being more observant of yourself, your surroundings, habits and people, places, and things that trigger stress and anxiety for you. You understand how and why we get attached and how detrimental it can be to hang on to habits, people, places, and things that are not beneficial for us. You will have some understanding of the attitudes of mindfulness and will have built up a bank of techniques to help bring calm and peace into your life. We have discussed how the stress response can be interrupted and that you can have control over the anxious feelings, sensations, and thoughts that have felt like they controlled you. They don't. You can't control all the thoughts that might pop into your head, but you can control how you respond to them and whether you act on them.

By grounding yourself in the here and now, fully being present in your own life, you can have some mastery over how you live and how you feel. You might experience sensations, reactions, or be aware of habits you want to change. As you adopt mindfulness practices and notice your own responses and behaviour, you might spot habits you want to let go of. Be open and willing to change. However, to effect change, one needs a plan. Acceptance is a key mindfulness attitude, but this does not mean you have to accept your feelings of stress and anxiety as a permanent state. By making changes, you are being compassionate towards yourself. You want a more peaceful, happier life experience and that will happen gently and gradually.

Be clear about your intentions. This is step one of the plan. Be clear about what it is you want to achieve. Perhaps you want to let go of distressing sensations or troubling memories.

Step two involves doing everything you can to work towards your intention. Remember, you are not a victim tossed about on the sea of life. You can set your course and adjust your sails as you move along. By being sensitive to the winds, weather, and sea conditions, you will reach your destination more quickly and easily. By making your plan, doing what you can with awareness, willingness, trust, curiosity, and patience with yourself and life, you will move forward.

Step three is about letting go. You are letting go of any fixed, narrow definition of the outcome. You can still make adjustments along the way. You can even devise an alternative plan if you want to. But let go of just exactly how the outcome will manifest itself. If you find step three difficult, you could try a mantra such as this:

"In this situation may the highest good be done for all."

By letting go of the exact details of how your intentions will be realized, you are freeing up more mental space and energy to get on with what you need to do now. By focusing on what you can do today, you are avoiding the perils of constantly worrying about the future or brooding about the past. If you are not sure what you can do next, ask yourself 'What is the next right thing I can do now?' Just do what you can for today and let the rest go. You need not sort out your entire life today. Just do what seems right for today. Some days it might be more than other days. By being mindful, practising techniques such as meditation, mindfulness movement, breathing, and bringing awareness and presence to each moment, you will be in a better state to make the right decisions about what to do next.

Stay open to the idea that our plans might turn out better than we had expected. Or our plans might seem to go off course, only to arrive at where we hoped to get to but taking a much more interesting route. Be open to change but have a plan.

The act of breathing is a constant practice in letting go. We can't hoard our breath. We must breathe out to take in a fresh breath. We must let go continually to make space for the fresh breath. Each day we can take some action towards our intentions and then let go. You cannot control every minor detail.

You might struggle with the concept that you are good enough as you are today. Perhaps you feel you need to make drastic changes, you need to improve, get better, or make more of yourself. Just play about with the idea that perhaps you are whole and complete exactly as you are today. You can still plan to make changes you wish for. You can do this mindfully and with compassion for yourself and others. As you take action, operate from a gentle acceptance of yourself. Do what you can to make changes that will be beneficial for you. All you need to do is take a few steps each day and the change will happen, if this is what you want. By taking these steps, keep your intentions in mind you will grow and develop.

As an example, think of a baby. The adults in a baby's life know the baby will grow, develop, and change because, if the baby is healthy and taken care of, this will happen naturally. The adults don't look at the baby, shake their heads, and make tutting noises. They don't sigh and worry that the baby is not enough because it cannot yet do everything. The adults accept that nature will take its course and the baby will develop the skills, abilities, and qualities that a fully grown human being will gain over time. The adults might make plans to facilitate the best education they can for the child. They might ensure they live in a pleasant and safe neighbourhood to ensure the child's best chances for a happy and healthy childhood. But sane and balanced adults don't plan every minute detail of how they think the child will turn out. They do the best they can and let life unfold. Using this as an analogy, you might do the best you can to work towards your intention or goal and then let life unfold. Let go of the precise outcomes. Trust the process.

Accept that experiencing a range of emotions is a rich part of the human experience and that we cannot eliminate all stress from our lives. So, if you do feel stressed, accept this as part of life, experience it mindfully, and bring compassion to the experience, doing what you can to alleviate the stress. We can be mindful of our feelings, reactions, and triggers, then make some adjustments of circumstances that are within our control, no matter how limited. We can focus on changing what we can to reduce stress and bring a fresh perspective to our stresses.

Focus on establishing habits and attitudes that cultivate peace and calm. These will help build a stable base to operate from. Reflect on your lifestyle and ask yourself if your choices are beneficial to creating a calm and peaceful life for yourself. Take a few moments to make a note of any practical changes you would like to make. This could be diet, exercise, how you spend free time, the amount of work you undertake, or getting help with tasks at home. You could also reflect on how you perceive feelings of stress or anxiety and re-frame them as natural response to a perceived threat. Re-evaluate the validity of the threat – is it real? Do what you can to minimise or ameliorate the threat and let the rest go.

Meditation 5: Peaceful Calmness.

To do this meditation, please ensure you are somewhere where you can see the sky. Sitting facing a window is great. If you can sit outside in nature, that would be even better. Do not stare straight at the sun.

Sit upright in a relaxed but upright position. Settle comfortably but keep your spine straight. Keep your eyes open but allow the gaze to be soft and unfocused. Keep your jaw relaxed and be aware of the feel of your tongue against the roof of your mouth and behind your teeth. Allow for some space between your upper and lower sets of teeth.

Gradually bring your attention to the breath. Notice if it is shallow or deep. Are you breathing into the upper chest area or into the abdomen? Is the breath fast or slow? Notice the air coming into the nose – does it feel cool? As the breath leaves the nose, how does that feel?

Move your attention to the shoulders and let them drop a little. Sweep your attention down the torso and into the area around the hips, buttocks, and thighs. Be aware of the sensations around this part of the body. Do you sense any heaviness in this area?

Move the attention down to the legs and feet. Notice how the feet feel on the floor. Where does the floor make contact with the feet?

Spend a few moments with your focus on the breath and the sensations in the body.

After a few moments, bring your attention to the view you can see through the window. Focus on the part of the sky that you can see. Notice what you see. Really look at the colour of the sky.

If it is a night-time sky, can you see the moon or stars? Perhaps you are in a town or city and the stars are obscured by city lights. Can you see the outlines of any clouds etched into the night-time sky?

If it is daytime, is the sky blue or grey? Can you see fluffy white clouds or grey rolling ones? Is the sky a solid grey with no individual clouds visible? Notice what the weather is doing today. Do you see any birds in the sky? Keep your focus on the patch of sky you can see, no matter how small this patch might be. Notice as many slight details as you can.

Now bring your attention to yourself. What effect do the sky and weather conditions have on you today? Do you notice any aversion or particular gratitude for what you see outside today? If the skyscape or weather brings up any memory or strong emotion, just notice it, label it as a 'just a thought' and let it go. No need to focus on any thoughts just now. Keep your attention on the body, breath, and the sky.

Reflect on the changing conditions of the sky and weather. You may have noticed a change in the sky. Perhaps there is a patch of blue appearing in a grey sky, or a break in night-time clouds revealing the moon, or perhaps the sky has darkened if it is moving towards evening.

Be conscious of the changeability of clouds, weather, and the sky itself. Notice how the sky is constantly changing, sometimes quickly, sometimes slowly, but it never stays the same for long. Reflect on the changeability of emotions and feelings. Notice your emotional state today. Name it and let the thought go. No need to analyse it just now. Notice how internal events such as memories, bodily sensations, or particular thoughts can influence feelings. Notice how external events or conditions can influence thoughts. No need to dwell on this, just notice your own emotions right now. Look at all this objectively, with compassion and kindness for yourself. Accept it as part of your total experience of the here and now. Accept it for what it is: something that will pass.

Bring your attention back to the breath. Breathe deep into the abdomen and keep your focus on the abdomen, fully experiencing the inflation and deflation of the belly. As you breathe in, focus on the word 'peace' and as you breathe out, focus on the word 'calm'. Continue to breathe in on 'peace' and out on 'calm' for a few moments. If you feel any agitation or disturbance, bring your attention back to the breath, and as you breathe out allow a small sigh to escape, releasing the tension.

Make space for what you feel right here and now and accept your feelings as they are today. Reflect on how they will change. Focus on fully experiencing them now, as they are.

On the next out-breath, begin gently to move the head. Tuck the chin in towards the chest and then look up towards the ceiling. Look over the left shoulder, then over the right shoulder. Roll the shoulders back and then forward. Focus on a detail you can see here in the room or close by and bring your attention to your immediate external environment. Slowly stand up, perhaps stretch gently, and carry on with your routine.

Chapter Six: Appreciation and Acceptance.

"The standard way of reducing stress in our culture is to put as much energy as possible into trying to arrive at a moment that matches our preferences. This ensures that we feel some measure of stress until we get there (assuming we ever will). Even worse, it makes the present moment an unacceptable place to be." – David Cain

***

Louise stood back from the window display she had been working on. Karen, her manager, approached her with a broad smile on her face. "Looking good, Louise!" she said.

Louise felt the warmth of a blush creeping up her neck and face but shook off her embarrassment and grinned back at her boss. Karen stood with her hands on her hips, surveying Louise's work, and continued, "I like the bunting and the way you have picked out our range of shoes to match the colour of our promotional banner – great job." As Karen rushed off to deal with a customer, she called over her shoulder, "Louise, will you do the window display for us in the main store in the city centre?" Louise nodded enthusiastically and give a thumbs up.

As she cleared away packaging and cardboard, Louise enjoyed a sense of gratitude for her work. Maybe this job would work out after all…

***

Rob's mum opened her front door slowly, peaking her nose around the door and looking at him warily. It took a few seconds for her to register that it was him. "Oh. It's you." She stood back and let him in. Rob had a key but always rang the bell out of courtesy. He noted that today her hair looked uncombed and her clothes were rumpled. He realized she was wearing the same clothes as yesterday. His mother moved slowly, catching on to items of furniture as she passed them to steady herself. Every movement looked like a supreme effort for her today.

At last, she reached her armchair and sat down heavily with a dramatic sigh. Rob could feel the familiar mixture of impatience and pity rise in his chest. He was aware of his breath quickening and could feel the thud of his heartbeat as he composed himself.

"Have you had any breakfast mum?" She was oddly quiet today and seemed distracted. "What? Mmm...I don't know." She looked off into the distance and shook her head. Rob took a few deep breaths and waited. As he breathed out, he tried to let go of the familiar tension that built up when dealing with his confused mother. He sat with her in silence and took in the heart-wrenching reality of the situation. However, this time he tried to consciously accept what was going on, and to do what he could to help his mother. "I'll just go and put the kettle on while you have a think, mum." She looked at him with a weak smile, "Okay, love, thanks."

***

Every day is a miracle. We wake up; we are alive. The delicate balance of our body and brain chemistry is aligned. Our organs are functioning. These are all things to appreciate before we even start our day.

In this chapter, we will look at appreciation and gratitude. Perhaps you baulk at gratitude or feel that there is little to appreciate in your circumstances. If you don't feel grateful and find it difficult to summon up an attitude of gratitude, just accept that is how it is for you today. Work on acceptance of your feelings and the situation you find yourself in. There is no need to force anything but keep an open mind. Perhaps in time you will see aspects of your life to be grateful for. Gratitude cannot be forced, but it can be gently cultivated. Even if you don't feel it, you could try some of the exercises coming up and your feelings might shift.

There is a subtle difference between appreciation and gratitude. Appreciation is the acknowledgment of the quality or value of something or someone. Gratitude is the feeling of being thankful for that thing or person. So, appreciation and gratitude go hand in hand. They are different and work together as a two-step process.

When we feel stressed and anxious, we are probably not feeling particularly appreciative or grateful for our current circumstances. If you have been or are going through a difficult time, this is perfectly understandable. You mustn't beat yourself up for not being grateful. Your mind, emotions, and body have probably been fixated on just getting you through the tough times.

Taking a few seconds to be grateful helps interrupt the stress response. You will remember that is the physiological and hormonal responses your body makes when you are feeling stressed: the quickening heartbeat, the rise in adrenalin and cortisol. These responses put us into fight, flight or freeze mode. The part of the brain that we use to organize ourselves and think things through logically switches off, and we react on pure instinct. By taking a few seconds to feel thankful or notice the good in a situation, we can give our thinking brains time to recover and make better decisions in a crisis. Just a few seconds, that's all it takes.

On a day-to-day basis, if we employ gratitude exercises and techniques, we can begin to reframe our situation. Most things are as good or bad as you think they are. By seeing aspects of your life that are positive or pleasurable, even an exceedingly demanding situation can be made more tolerable. It can make the difference between misery and growth. You are not pushing any feelings or memories away, but it can give some hope if you can see your circumstances and experiences in terms of growth and development. This concept of growth following on from a difficult experience is encouraging, so let's look at an approach called 'Post Traumatic Growth'.

This book is not specifically aimed at people who are suffering with PTSD. Post-Traumatic Stress Disorder is a condition that can take years to work through. If you are suffering from PTSD you must get the help you need. Don't try to go it alone. However, there has been hope for people who suffer from PTSD in recent times. That hope has come in the form of 'Post Traumatic Growth', which is seeing the potential for growth that could come from the traumatic experience. This is a shift in focus from what has gone wrong to what can be gained. I mention it here as the approaches listed below can be helpful in dealing with stress or anxiety. Seeing a difficult experience in terms of what you can learn from it can give a sense of meaning to the suffering.

A difficult or traumatic experience can crystalize values and remind us of what is most important in our lives. It can help put life into perspective and urge us to reach out to others and forge connections. There are five recommended ways to foster growth after experiencing trauma: One is to plan enjoyable activities. Two is to define your values and see how you can practice and implement these values in your life. Three is to get involved in the local community in some way that you would enjoy. Four is to set goals that are realistic and specific. Five is to validate your experience, emotions, and to not rush the process, as it will take time.

In working through these steps, you can begin to turn a traumatic experience around and discover what you enjoy, value, and want to achieve. By making some efforts each day to focus on what you appreciate and are grateful for, you can begin to plan for a growth response rather than being caught in a loop of reliving trauma and feeling trapped by it.

By planning things you enjoy, you can begin to see that life is worth living. Conversely, by focusing on the trauma and not being in the present moment, it is easy to lose touch with whatever would once have given you pleasure and enjoyment. So, feel the emotions and give yourself time but keep your focus on the present moment, which is the first step in cultivating appreciation and gratitude. If you are constantly ruminating about the past or worrying about the future, you leave no space to appreciate the present moment.

Right now, look around, take a breath in, listen to what is going on near you, feel the texture of the material closest to your hands, and be aware of any sensations in your body. At regular points, take a few seconds to stop, look, and listen. This is life. This is all we have, moment by moment – a whole string of moments that make up what our life is. Don't miss out on it.

Waking up each day could be an exercise in appreciation and gratitude: an appreciation of a warm, comfortable bed, a roof over your head, and that you are alive and breathing. By being fully present, you can find other aspects of your existence to appreciate and feel thankful for. If you don't feel thankful, be gentle with yourself. Just rest in appreciation of something that is most meaningful to you. This could take seconds. You don't even need to get out of bed.

As you move through your day, find little aspects of the day to feel some gratitude for. This could be breakfast, or a particularly nice cup of coffee, or the fact that your kitchen cupboards contain food. The things to be grateful for do not need to be dramatic or grandiose. Often it is the little things in life that make the most difference. Actively seek out experiences and aspects of your day to appreciate. To do this, you need to be fully present to what the day brings. By being fully present in the here and now, you won't have the time or mental space to continually worry about the future or ruminate on the past. You might notice things you didn't even see before.

I remember some years ago actively practising gratitude after a period of feeling overwhelmed by life events including bereavement. I realized that to move forward I needed to focus on the present with a sense of appreciation for what I enjoyed about my life at the time. After just a couple of days of harnessing this attitude of gratitude in my life, I realized I had a lovely garden. The season was just moving from a chilly English spring into an abundant early summer. I can clearly remember looking out of the window and being struck by the astounding vibrancy and beauty of the garden. How had I not seen this before? I was stuck in a dark place of sadness and grief but by gently turning towards what I could feel grateful for, my mind-set began to shift.

Mindfulness practices do not have to be complicated or time-consuming. Simply by being in the present and adopting attitudes such as appreciation and gratitude, you can begin to have some serenity and calm in your life.

You might want to practise more formal gratitude exercises. If you feel you have the time, these are wonderful exercises to build into your daily routine. Here are some suggestions:

Keep a gratitude journal. This could be a special notebook, reserved to record what you feel grateful for. Just note down a few observations each day. By writing them down, you have a record to look at when you are feeling stressed, anxious, or just feeling discouraged.

Another simple practice is to have a gratitude jar. You can use any jar for this, but if you want to decorate a jar and make it special, that would be even better. All you need to do is write down what you are grateful for on a slip of paper and pop it into the jar. See the jar fill up. This is a lovely exercise to do as a family and will help your children build attitudes of appreciation and gratitude too.

This next practice can be done anywhere at any time and only takes a moment – gratitude prompts. At points in the day, bring your focus entirely to the present moment and go through this mental list of gratitude prompts:

I am grateful for these three things I can see…

I am grateful for these three things I can hear…

I am grateful for these three things I can touch and feel…

I am grateful for these three things I can smell…

I am grateful for these three things I can taste.

Keep a pebble or rock where you can see it at regular points during the day. When you notice it, think of something you are grateful for in that moment. A friend of mine keeps a special bead hanging up in the rear-view mirror of her car. When she sees the bead hanging, it reminds her to recall something she is grateful for.

If you have children at home, play gratitude games. For example, over dinner in the evening go around everyone at the table and ask them to tell you one thing they are grateful for.

Going for a gratitude walk is another simple practice that can easily be built into your day. Walk mindfully and slowly around your neighbourhood or through a park or along a beach. Fully experience the walk and really notice what your senses pick up on. Focus on the aspects of your walk you feel gratitude for.

Gratitude reflection: this could be while waiting in line, or stuck in traffic, or doing a routine chore. Just take a few moments to reflect on what you appreciate about that moment and experience a sense of gratitude. For example, whilst washing the dishes: gratitude for hot running water, for the soap, for the meal you have just enjoyed, for pretty crockery, for the ability to stand at the sink, to see the bubbles in the water and hear the rush of the water, and enjoy the sensation of warm soapy water on your hands.

Writing a letter or email of appreciation to a friend or family member is a practice that will foster stronger connections with others. This will help you appreciate this person in your life, feel gratitude, and enjoy bringing some joy and positivity into some else's life.

At regular points in the day, take a moment to appreciate yourself and your strengths, accomplishments, and skills. Mentally compliment yourself. This can be hard, especially if you tend to be very self-critical, but it will get easier with practice. Start with small things. For example, praise yourself if you prepared a delicious meal or pushed yourself a little out of you comfort zone. When you have some time, sit down with your journal and make a list of everything you can think of that you are proud of. Keep the list to look back on when you feel you can't cope, or you are feeling low about yourself. This will help you build resilience to deal with life's challenges.

Some people find the use of gratitude apps helps remind them to focus on what makes them grateful. These apps will flash up a reminder to record what you are grateful for that day.

The above are just some suggestions. You might think of more. The important thing is to pick out one or two things you know you can do. Plan when you will do them and practice them consistently.

***

Life's challenges might come in the form of people, circumstances, or setbacks. How we view our challenges is crucial. Bring attitudes of appreciation and acceptance to the challenge. If we do our best to re-frame difficulties into opportunities for growth, we make room for a more optimistic outlook and can find some meaning in life events. Accept that life brings challenges. No one can totally avoid them.

When faced with a setback or challenge, bring your awareness to how you feel in your body. Notice where you are holding on to tension in the body. Stretch and move to avoid tension building up and causing more problems.

Breathe. If you become anxious when thinking about the breath, just breathe deeply and slowly. But if you are comfortable focusing on the breath, you could try to practise a short breathing exercise such as box breathing. It is called box breathing as the breath follows a pattern of four, like the four lines of a box. What you do is breath in for four counts, hold for four counts, breathe out for four, and hold for four – then repeat for a few moments until you feel calmer.

If someone has just delivered unwelcome news and needs a response, don't feel pressured to answer right away. Ask for more time if needed. Tell them you need some time and will get back to them as soon as you can.

If you are facing a disappointment or setback, accept that sometimes you don't know why things happen as they do. Continually asking yourself 'why?' can put you into an endless loop of over-analysing and being self-critical. Accept what has happened and that you don't know why.

Focus on the present and what you can do to make the situation a better outcome for yourself.

If someone has challenged you in some way, don't be tempted to immediately retaliate, fight, or argue. This will rarely have a satisfactory outcome. You can behave with dignity and acceptance, even if you don't like what has happened. Take some time to think about what to do next.

You know that mindfulness is not about drifting aimlessly, so make a plan. You can put thought and effort into devising a plan to overcome a challenge. Do this with the best interests of all at heart. Act with compassion and willingness to grow and move forward.

Accept your feelings and honour them. Dealing with a situation as best you can in an honest and forthright way relieves you of daily indecision and the anxiety produced by avoidance. For example, if you have racked up a huge credit card debt, contact the card company and make a plan with them. This means you will have more time and energy to move forward with your plans rather than being constantly worried about how you are going to pay back such a large debt.

When you feel overwhelmed by worry, bring your mind back to the present moment. Look around and be grateful for three things you are experiencing at that moment.

Take pleasure in any creative projects you enjoy. If you enjoy cooking, immerse yourself in that – or playing an instrument or sewing or painting. Find an outlet to channel your energy and attention. This will avoid getting into a downward cycle of rumination and worry that goes nowhere.

Focus on one thing at a time and avoid multi-tasking, no matter how rushed you feel. By trying to do too much in a short space of time, you will feel more overwhelmed and pressured. You will probably also make mistakes and get into a downward spiral of frustration and agitation.

Get out into nature. If you are in a situation in which you are under constant stress, it is important to build in regular doses of activities to help alleviate the stress. Being in nature is a proven way to reduce stress and anxiety. Scientists have identified elements in nature that act beneficially on the brain to soothe the nervous system.

Forgive and let go. Try not to hold on to resentments about the part played by other people. Look at their actions with compassion. This includes yourself. If you have acted in a way that you consider to be unwise, foolish, or ill-advised, forgive yourself, learn what you can from the experience and plan to move forward. See forgiveness as a way of remaining connected with people. Tend to friendships and connections, and ask for help if you need it. This is not a sign of weakness. It delights most people to be trusted to help or to just listen.

Know that everything will pass, whether you label it good or bad. By resisting and struggling with what is in the present, we just make the process much more painful. Look at any areas of resistance you may have. Allow a sense of space and acceptance around your resistance. Don't feel that you need to shoe-horn yourself into accepting something that you really baulk at. Practice willingness to accept something as best you can for now. Whilst practising willingness, you can plan to move forward, enlisting help if needed. Keep taking little steps. If faced with doubt or uncertainty, just ask yourself: what is the next right thing you can do to improve the situation for all those affected by it? You do not need to rush or stress. The best decisions are seldom made in either of these states.

Showing yourself some self-care can be a hard thing to do, especially if you feel you need to be constantly doing things for other people or have limited time. But these very patterns of thought are symptoms of anxiety and stress, so even more reason to fit in some self-care. By ignoring your own needs and having no appreciation of yourself, how can you show gratitude or appreciation for anyone else? By continually driving ourselves into the ground with endless to-do lists and rushing around worrying about others, how can we be fully present in our own lives or the lives of those around us?

Perhaps your pattern of anxiety is a more lonely, isolated experience. Perhaps your anxious thoughts are orientated on yourself and you feel trapped in an endless cycle of worry about your health, future, finances, or relationships. If this is the case, you might look at practical things you are doing for yourself to help you feel better. Self-care could take the form of looking at your nutrition. Do you cook proper meals for yourself? Try focusing on cooking a nutritious and enjoyable meal, something simple like fixing a salad or a sandwich made with delicious and colourful ingredients, then set a place for yourself at the table and use your best tableware. Is there someone you could invite to share the meal with? Doing something that others will appreciate can help overcome isolation.

By doing pleasant, resourcing things for ourselves, we help establish a positive loop of trigger, behaviour, reward. If, when you get hungry, you usually eat something to hand like a bag of crisps or half a packet of biscuits, after the initial buzz of salt or sugar, you feel worse. But by preparing a nutritious meal and making a small effort, you feel better for eating some healthy, enjoyable food and your positive emotions are the reward to repeat this more healthful behaviour.

In the next chapter, we will look in detail at a whole host of other self-care actions. Sometimes the act of self-care takes more discipline than we apply to our work life. Self-care is not just about massages and spas. Perhaps push yourself gently to go for a swim or out for a walk or set aside ten minutes to organize your desk – these are activities that will ultimately make you feel better.

In Appendix 5 there are lists of self-care activities to consider if you need some ideas to get started. If you have been routinely neglecting yourself it can be hard to think of things you would find uplifting, relaxing, and refreshing. So, pick out some activities to try soon.

This is not selfish. By doing things for yourself that are sustaining, enriching, and healthful, you are building yourself up to be calm, purposeful, and useful to yourself and others.

***

"In mindfulness, acceptance always comes first, change comes after." – Shamash Aldina.

***

Let's be clear that acceptance is not the same as resignation. Resignation has a connotation of being defeated. Acceptance is about embracing things as they are and is an active process. You are *choosing* to accept something. You can then begin to discern what you have some control over and plan to change what you can and accept the rest.

When we accept things just as they are, we are taking the first step to being fully aware of our difficulties. We can then take action to respond to those difficulties rather than reacting on autopilot. When we react in a knee-jerk fashion, we are running old, conditioned programs of behaviour that are unhelpful and do not initiate any true change.

Acceptance is the first step to realize change. Acceptance could mean accepting our current life situation but using it as a springboard to plan change and development.

Acceptance could be on a more micro-scale, such as accepting our feelings in each moment and looking calmly and dispassionately at how we are feeling without necessarily trying to change it right away, even if these feelings are perceived as unpleasant or negative. Much can be learned from accepting feelings and just sitting with the feeling. Don't get too caught up in analysing or asking why – just notice and let the feeling go. You can then actively choose to do something that is nurturing and comforting for you.

Try it. Recall a recent situation you have felt upset about. It could be a rejection, resentment, or fear. Just sit with the thought of it. Notice the feelings that come up. Avoid ruminating or having conversations in your head about it. Just look at it with interest and compassion for yourself.

By accepting and not resisting the feeling, it can lose its power over us. We can then take steps to do something healthy and constructive to change the feeling if we choose to. We could choose a meaningful activity to get involved with, do some mindful movement, meditate, read, journal, or breathe. We could attend to our biological needs, such as hunger, thirst, or rest; or our psychological needs, such as for company or an outlet to talk. Music and laughter are powerful too. Have a playlist of songs that cheer you up or a favourite comedy show. All this helps lift a negative mood.

Without that first crucial step of acceptance of the feeling we perceive to be negative, the choices we make to change the feeling could be much less healthy. We will probably go into our automatic programming and attack the biscuit tin (cookie jar), yell at someone, kick the dog, hit the bar, or pick up a cigarette. Being present, experiencing your feelings, and making conscious and deliberate choices will help us to find equilibrium and a happier balance.

In the next chapter we will look at a cornerstone of mindfulness – compassion – and discuss self-care in more detail.

Meditation 6: Appreciation.

Sitting or lying comfortably, allow your thoughts to settle. Bring your awareness to the breath. Be conscious of the movement of air into the nostrils; be aware of any slight flaring of the nostrils as you breathe in. Just notice the breath. Notice the sensations around the face as you breathe in. Do not alter anything unnecessarily, just take note. Be aware of any tension in the jaw area or between the brows. Notice if there is any tension or feelings of fatigue around the eyes or eyelids. With a sense of curiosity, focus on how your temples feel and the top of the head. Be aware of how the whole head feels and focus with gratitude on how the delicate muscles, bones, and ligaments in the neck and upper spine support the weight of the head.

Slide your awareness down the spine to the area around the hips and seat. Breathe into this area. Feel grounded and secure as you sit or lie. Be aware of any tightness in this area. Have a sense of the weight in this area and be thankful for feeling grounded and secure in your body.

Bring the awareness back to the breath. Breathe deeply into the chest cavity. Let the breath be gentle and soft, without force. Stay with the breath here a few moments.

With a focus on the area around the heart, continue breathing in gently but deeply and letting the air escape gradually, emptying the lungs fully, pausing for a second as the lungs are empty, enjoying a sense of stillness and calm. Letting the air just trickle out of the nostrils, imagine breathing up and down the spine, up to the head, and back down to the hips.

Have a sense of gratitude for all that your body and mind can do. Imagine the breath washing over the top of the head, relaxing any tension or scattered thoughts, and coming back down the spine, easing any aches, stress, or discomfort in the back area. Focus on the back and recall all the movements the back can make, the daily twists, bends, and stretches your spine needs to make to carry out your everyday activities. Have a deep sense of appreciation for all that you can do. Accept any limitations you may have at this time. If there is pain or discomfort, breathe into the discomfort, and relax as you breathe out. Let the entire upper body relax, but if sitting upright maintain an erect and dignified posture.

Bringing the attention back now to the heart area. Imagine a sense of warmth around the heart. Breathe into this. Be aware of the feelings and sensations around the heart area. If you notice a sense of appreciation, peace, or joy, focus on this. Perhaps today, this is not accessible, if not just keep your focus on the heart area and recall the words peace and joy. Breathe in peace and breathe out joy. Behind your closed eyes imagine a screen without pictures, but you see a golden glow. Have a sense of this glow and warmth that is radiating up from your heart. Continue to breathe in peace and breathe out joy. Relax with this sense of peace and joy as you keep your focus on the breath and on the warm glow that is emanating from your heart. Enjoy this stillness for a few moments.

Now, with your eyes still closed, recall a picture of the room you are in. Envisage the room in detail. Be aware of any sounds in the room. Deepen the breath right down into the abdomen and rotate the head gently, releasing the back of the neck. Rotate your shoulders and move your hands and feet, perhaps making some small circles with the hands and feet. Once more, breathe in peace and breathe out joy. On the out-breath, open your eyes and smile. Put your right hand over your heart and have a sense of gratitude for the life and vitality in your body, smile, breathe into the heart area and on the out-breath, stand up slowly, and carry on with your activities, taking with you a sense of joy and gratitude.

Chapter Seven: Compassion.

"Look at other people and ask yourself if you are really seeing them or just your thoughts about them." – Jon Kabat-Zinn.

***

"Who is it visiting today?" Rob's mother searched his face with her rheumy eyes, a cup of tea perched in front of her as they sat in her immaculate living room.

For about the tenth time that morning, Rob responded, "it's the doctor, mum." He felt the usual irritation at her repetitive questions but answered her calmly and quietly. Letting go of any expectation that the situation would be any different today.

"But I'm not ill." Rob did not respond. "I'M NOT ILL," she repeated, much more loudly.

"I know. It's just a check-up, mum." He had rehearsed what he would say, knowing she would resist seeing the doctor. After discussing her situation with the group the previous week, he had agreed he would seek some help with his mum, so he had arranged for the doctor to visit to do an assessment. Rob's heart lifted a little and he felt better today than he had in a long time, which gave him the ability to deal with his mother's constant repetitive questions kindly and patiently.

***

Louise stood outside the large, metal gate of the dog rescue centre. Her heart thumped rapidly, and she worried about how she might come across to the centre's manager. Interviews of any kind terrified her. She would stumble over her words and stammer, or just completely freeze. Before Louise had time to dwell anymore on her interview nerves, the gate scrapped open and a woman, probably in her early fifties, in dirty corduroy trousers and grubby shirt greeted Louise. 'Hi, I'm Sarah. Come in, come in.' She juggled a bucket in one hand and a scrubbing brush in the other. Sarah strode ahead of Louise, glancing back to ensure the gate was secured before opening a second gate.

Louise trotted behind Sarah trying to keep up with her as Sarah spoke rapidly, outlining the history to the centre and the duties undertaken by volunteers. Louise needn't have worried about what she was going to say as Sarah did all the talking. Louise looked around at the dogs, some in small pens, some on their own in kennels behind wire gates.

Louise loved dogs and found them much easier to be around than people. She had agreed with her sister, Vikki, that she would branch out and do more with her life than work, worry, and watch soap operas. Sarah was obviously grateful for all help received and only asked a few basic questions. Back at the gate on the way out, Louise agreed she would volunteer at the rescue centre every Sunday afternoon. Walking to her car, she felt much more buoyant and hopeful than she had in a long time.

***

A core attitude in the practice of mindfulness is compassion for everybody and everything, including yourself. As we discuss compassion in this chapter, please do not beat yourself up for beating yourself up! If you notice that you criticize yourself harshly, or have judgemental, unkind thoughts come up about other people, well done on noticing it. You are being mindful and becoming aware of your thoughts and reactions. This is a helpful and positive thing. Instead of judging yourself harshly, see the thought for what it is – just a random notion that has popped into your mind – and kindly set an intention to foster some compassion for that person or that situation. As this chapter progresses, we will talk about practical ways to do this.

Compassion is not pity, whether that is for yourself or someone else. Compassion is empathetic, warm, and supportive. It is an attitude of coming alongside someone in an encouraging and understanding way, not looking down on them or feeling sorry for them.

Being compassionate makes us feel good, it enhances our self-esteem and the concept of ourselves. In looking at what drives peoples' behaviour, Dr Jud Brewer has studied the effects of kindness.[1] In a nutshell, he has looked at how behaviour triggers the reward centres in the brain. He has shown how being kind triggers pleasant sensations, the sort of feel-good response we get from eating chocolate or getting a 'like' on Facebook. So, the associations we build up by being kind become positive and reinforce our desire to be kind. Therefore, once you start, it gets easier. And you can 'fake it to make it.' You can be compassionate even if you don't feel it. The feeling will follow the action, so don't wait until you feel a wave of compassion to wash over you before you start treating yourself and other people with kindness.

The more we practise being genuinely kind, the better we feel. Being kind benefits the giver as much as the receiver. Such acts give us a sense of connectedness with others. We feel less alone, less anxious, and fearful. In this chapter, I will explain why that is and what we can do to help lift ourselves out of the isolation, fear, and anxiety we might be experiencing. Feeling more connected with others is a sign that mindfulness is working in our lives.

We might think we would intuitively know what we mean by compassion and kindness. However, a few years back an item on the news caught my attention. Apparently, compassion is now a subject taught on the university curriculum for student nurses. It surprised me that this should be a skill that needed to be taught. Surely, anyone who was interested in being a nurse and helping others would be a naturally compassionate person? I was wrong in my thinking.

Often as adults, we can get so caught up in the rush and pressure of life and lose connection with the quietness of the heart that prompts us to be compassionate and kind towards others and ourselves. We can get so enmeshed in the daily grind of making a living, paying bills, meeting deadlines, and keeping the wheels of our lives turning that making time to be compassionate seems almost irrelevant. Sometimes we need to remind ourselves to be kind. Compassion doesn't just happen.

This is where mindfulness is so beneficial. By looking at our own lives and those of others with a genuine spirit of kindness and compassion, we see and connect with what is in front of us. When we are distracted by worries, concerns, and negative feelings, we won't have this sense of connection or awareness.

If we are not mindful, we can drift into indifference and being judgemental. Then harshness can creep in. This hard attitude fosters many unhealthy and unhelpful behaviours towards us and others. We might get locked into our own sense of suffering, closing ourselves in a prison of victimhood, unable to help ourselves or anyone else. We might feel a sour attitude towards the success of others and gravitate towards unpleasant news and complaints. We become reactive and angry.

Research carried out at the University of Michigan by Sarah Konrath has shown how as a society we are becoming less compassionate.[2] She has examined studies that were made between 1979 and 2009 of 13,000 college students, Konrath discovered that self-reported concern for the welfare of others was steadily declining, particularly from the early 1990s. Alarmingly, rates of compassion are at their lowest levels for thirty years and are continuing to decline.

Interestingly, these figures appear to correlate with an increase in levels of stress and anxiety.

Practising compassion helps us to identify with others and lifts us out of isolation and a sense of lonely suffering. We realize that suffering is part of the human condition. As we identify strongly with others, we feel more of a sense of being in this together. This sense of identity and togetherness is important. As human beings, we are hard-wired to feel part of the tribe. It is an ancient and deep-rooted alarm system that goes off when we feel isolated or on edge. By feeling part of humanity, we feel connected and bonded with others. If we practise compassion with an open heart, we will feel the benefits in terms of a sense of belonging, a feeling of peace and calm, and enhanced self-esteem. Hopefully, our acts of kindness and compassion will help others, so it is a win-win situation.

Compassion is beneficial for our physical health as well as out emotional and mental health. Dr David Hamilton looked at how being kind is good for our heart [3]. Being kind releases a hormone called oxytocin, the 'hug drug'. Oxytocin is the hormone that helps us feel connected to others. Besides this positive effect, this also helps to strengthen our heart health. When the hormone is released, the blood vessels in the heart dilate (open up) easing any stress on the heart muscle.

When practising compassion, it is worth bearing in mind that when we are being considerate or of service, we genuinely aim to enhance the lives of others. We are not seeking approval or validation from others. This might be a pleasant side-effect but try to be motivated by a sense of doing your best for someone else for its own sake. Your worth as a person does not depend on the opinion or validation of others. Work on building up your own opinion of yourself. You can hold yourself in high regard as someone who is kind, compassionate, and considerate of others. The other person need not show you gratitude or appreciation. Some people might not even notice and as your practice grows, you might feel motivated to be randomly kind in anonymous ways, because you feel better when you practice kindness.

No one else will know, but the important thing here is that *you* know.

When we talk about practising compassion, what does that mean? What does it look like?

Some years ago, when I attended some training related to meditation, I formed close bonds with the other participants on the course. I realized that the key reason I had formed these friendships was that people listened mindfully to each other. They were present. There were not the usual interruptions and crosstalk that go on amongst groups of friends. Giving someone our complete attention, being present and listening is one of the most compassionate acts we can build into our daily lives. Here are some other examples of how you can practise compassion for yourself and others:

Small acts of kindnesses in the form of courtesies to strangers when driving or moving about. This could be as simple as giving way to another driver or letting a car out in front of you in a queue of busy traffic or helping someone you can see is struggling. Don't worry if they don't wave or say thank you. Remind yourself you are doing this for yourself as well as other people. Give them some slack, perhaps they are concentrating on the traffic or distracted by their own thoughts or are involved in conversation with a passenger.

Most people love to get a phone call from someone just to ask how their day has been or receiving a note or card of appreciation. So, keep in touch with loved ones with regular calls, and communication. Simple acts such as making someone a hot drink, or a meal are small but powerful ways to show you care. Adopting attitudes of patience and acceptance by avoiding retaliating when irritated with someone, being patient with an elderly or infirm person and allowing yourself and others to make mistakes, are compassionate responses to situations that might otherwise make you feel frazzled and stressed. Accept that human beings are not perfect – and that includes you. Accept situations as they unfold. Of course, you can still act, but you will be doing so from a grounded, calm centre, responding in the best possible way.

Compassion is best practised daily, and not just reserved for those we love, pity, or naturally feel compassionate towards. Compassion is an unconditional practice. Even with particularly challenging people, we can understand that those in the most pain often try to inflict the most pain on others. This does not mean putting up with abusive or disrespectful behaviour – you have a duty to yourself to keep yourself safe – but you can bring a spirit of compassion to the situation by seeing it in these terms.

If you struggle with developing compassion or have difficulties in showing compassion for certain people, that is understandable. The important thing is that you are becoming aware of any difficulties you might have with practising compassion. You might just want to meditate and reflect on what compassion means to you for now and notice how you react towards others in pain, discomfort, or difficulties. Perhaps you feel nothing. Perhaps you feel distaste or irritation. Just notice these reactions without judging yourself. Meditating on compassion might seem like a self-centred occupation, but it will help to get your started and keep you going. Research shows that meditation can help us to become more compassionate, as meditation stimulates the areas of the brain responsible for a sense of social affiliation.[4] This is significant because studies have revealed that by connecting with others in a social and empathetic way, we can sustain compassion and active concern, so meditation helps us to become more compassionate and maintain compassion in the longer term. Therefore, use the guided meditations and your personal quiet time to help build your compassion 'muscle'.

If you struggle to practise compassion, start with something easy. Just be as kind and considerate as you can when out and about. Smile and be polite to strangers. If they don't smile back or don't appear to appreciate your act of kindness, remind yourself that you are practising this for yourself and wish them well. By acting kindly, you will feel better about yourself.

When out, perhaps when standing in line or waiting somewhere, really observe the people you see. Reflect on the fact that every person has a story to tell. They all have their worries, fears, joys, and sorrows. This is part of the human condition.

You might have embedded the attitude of compassion into your daily life and feel that it is easy to be kind towards others. Perhaps you are the person who is always looking out for others to the detriment of your own health and wellbeing. Perhaps you feel that this compulsion to help others has contributed to your stress and anxiety. You might be in a situation of having to care for others, maybe young children or an elderly relative. You might feel that the burdens of care placed on your shoulders have created unbearable stress for you. If this above applies to you, please get some support. No one should be alone in dealing with the emotional, physical, or financial strain that full-time caring can bring on. There are practical steps you can take such as enlisting the help of other family members or friends, approaching state or charitable bodies that could help, and ensuring you receive any benefits or financial support available.

In terms of mindfulness, if you are feeling overwhelmed, prioritize what you need to do every day. Instil a sense of curiosity, noticing your reactions and feelings without judgment. For instance, if you feel irritation with a toddler because he has thrown his diner across the kitchen again, be gentle with yourself as well as the child. Be aware of how you are feeling. The best compassion practice you can do is to focus on your behaviour and act in a kind and considerate way. You may not feel compassion, but just do your best – you can't force a compassionate feeling.

We all need to practise self-compassion. This is not selfish or self-centred. A harsh attitude towards ourselves can so easily spill over into a harshness that is directed at others. Later in this chapter, we will look at practical ways in which you can practise self-compassion and self-care.

In the past, I have seen in myself how, when I have felt overworked and underappreciated, I have been less tolerant towards others. It felt like the harder I pushed myself and struggled to keep going, the less patience I had with others. It was an attitude of 'I am getting on with it, why can't you!' This was not helpful for me or the other person and I was digging myself deeper into a hole of exhaustion, victimhood, and overwhelm.

Self-compassion is not a pity party. If you feel sorry for yourself, take some time to experience that. Have a brief cry to yourself if that helps. Write in your journal or talk to a trusted friend. Sit with the feeling and practise a loving-kindness meditation, such as the one included in this book. Feel a sense of acceptance for yourself and others. Accept all the myriad of feelings and sensations that might come up, just watching them without becoming too attached to what you notice. Do something kind for yourself and something kind for another person and then see how you feel.

Most human beings are very self-critical. This self-criticism seems to be hard-wired into our mental make-up. By observing your thoughts and responses you will become more aware of your own inner critic. Watch it, but don't attach any importance to what it says. Remember, shame might work in the short-term to change behaviour, but it will not last. Compassionate encouragement is more likely to sustain long term behaviour change, if you feel you need it.

The voice of the inner critic is a bit like a radio station, you can tune into it and listen to it, it might be on constantly in the background, it might have different programs such as 'I am useless' or 'I always make mistakes.' Or 'I am going to mess up'. By seeing these statements as random thoughts you do not need to attach any importance to them. By being aware of them for what they are, they are less likely to affect you in terms of creating anxiety, self-doubt, or flagging self-confidence. You can even thank your inner critic for the opinion and reassure yourself that you are not useless or that, yes, you do make mistakes sometimes, but everyone makes mistakes sometimes.

You can show yourself some compassion by attending to your self-care. In the last chapter, we looked at activities that might be resourcing or non-resourcing for you. Activities that make you feel drained, anxious, or ashamed are non-resourcing. Activities that help you feel refreshed, uplifted, and optimistic about life are resourcing. As well as your activities, consider your environment. Does it help you to feel calm, refreshed, and peaceful? You may be in a work environment over which you have little control. Perhaps it is noisy or busy. If this is the case, during the day try to have regular quick breaks to enjoy some peace. Try to get out for a brief walk at lunchtime and avoid eating hunched over your desk.

If you are in your home environment, try to create a calm, pleasant space as best you can. Avoid having the television or radio constantly on. Enjoy silence. Use music to create an ambient atmosphere. If you have young children at home, try to keep one room in the house where you know you can retreat to for some peace and quiet. Also, involve your children in being mindful. Encourage them to seek out and enjoy quiet, calm activities too.

Coming up next is a short exercise to complete to help you evaluate your current balance of self-care activities and plan in some necessary self-care. You will need something to write with and a sheet of paper or you could use a page in your journal. On the sheet of paper draw a line horizontally across the middle of the page. Next, draw two vertical lines down the page, equally spaced so that you have created six boxes on your sheet of paper. Then write a heading in each box. The six headings are:

Physical

Emotional

Social

Spiritual

Intellectual

Personal and domestic

What you will do next is write at least one activity or action in each box that you can do over the next week or so. Some things might be on-going, and some might be one-offs. Revisit and refresh your boxes regularly and write in your self-care activities onto your calendar, diary, or a phone app. The heading that you find most difficult to think of something to write under is probably the activity you need to do as a priority. For example, I regularly exercise and for me this is a natural part of my weekly activities, but I 'forget' to sort out the inbox for my e-mails.

The following is a list of some ideas to consider. There are more suggestions in Appendix 5 at the back of this book.

Under physical well-being, you could consider movement (walking, jogging, horse-riding, dancing, cycling, and swimming), sleep and rest (including naps and good sleep hygiene), food and hydration, limits on screen time, a massage, a haircut, a facial, or a hot shave.

Attending to your emotional needs might include activities such as being present most of the time, taking time out just to be, slowing down, writing in a journal, pausing to appreciate the present moment, doing kind acts, acknowledging emotions, practising attitudes of mindfulness like compassion and gratitude, silence, alone-time, or hugging a loved one or a pet.

Possible social activities could be ringing a friend or loved one, writing a letter, card, or email, sending some photos, giving a small gift, joining a club or society, starting or taking part in a self-help group.

Spiritual activities can be anything that you personally find inspiring such as getting out into nature, reading inspirational books, attending church or a consciousness-raising group, spending time with animals, listening to uplifting talks and podcasts, watching nature documentaries, even something as simple as looking at the stars and moon at night or looking up at the sky every day.

Find intellectual activities that are meaningful, enjoyable, and stimulating for you. Don't be tempted to take up activities because you think you should, or to impress anyone else. You might be interested in learning a language, reading, games, quizzes, teaching a skill, learning a skill, playing a sport that requires mental effort such as golf, setting goals, working out a route for a trip, or learning to play an instrument.

Personal activities are those that are centred on your personal living space or how you spend your time or plan for the future. Such activities could involve organizing a closet or drawer, cleaning and tidying, washing the car, being aware of finances and setting financial goals, writing realistic to-do lists, keeping an agenda, setting career goals, applying for a new job, applying for a course of study, or planning for a vacation.

What you should end up with is a grid filled with ideas for self-care activities. The first time you look at that grid, it might seem too much to take in. But that's easily solved. Have a good look at what you have written and ask yourself which one would, if you acted on it now, would have the biggest beneficial impact on your wellbeing and peace of mind. Put a circle around it. Then go and do something about it. Louise cracked on with arranging some voluntary work. Rob made an appointment to get help for his mother. What about you? What can you do that will make a difference?

Then, when you are satisfied you have attended to that act of self-care, go back to your grid and choose the next most important or urgent item. In this way, you can focus on sorting out your life step by step, which keeps this project manageable, and by doing it in order of importance, you ensure that you get the biggest results quickly, which will inspire you to carry on.

Your self-care ideas will need to fit in with your likes, abilities, and personality. More introverted people will need more alone-time than extroverts, who need lots of opportunities to be with others. Try to attain a balance that works for you. Start small. Make steady, consistent efforts, and keep it simple.

By attending to your self-care, you will be less bothered by sensations that you might perceive as anxiety such as feeling shaky or weak because you haven't eaten well or getting anxious about making mistakes because you are tired. Feeling well across all areas of life will give you the strength and confidence to deal with whatever life throws at you. Just knowing this can help ease anxiety.

Dealing with difficult people can be one of the biggest challenges that life can present and a source of ongoing stress and anxiety. I am sure you can think of at least one person in your life who you dread dealing with. This could be in your family, neighbourhood, or at work. Dealing with these people can make practising compassion particularly challenging.

Our perception of whom or what we consider difficult can be very subjective. Our own opinion of what we consider difficult from one day to the next might vary. What we consider being difficult can be affected by our own physical, emotional, and mental state. This can be in terms of how we perceive people, and in how we respond.

For example, do you remember the personal example I gave of a relative I considered to be difficult, who made comments about my son's television viewing habits? I considered this relative to be difficult in the sense of being opinionated and rude, but I had enough composure to let my initial reactions settle and consider what he said. After some reflection I realized that he was not being rude or opinionated, he was reacting to the information my son presented. He was not being difficult at all. Later, I could make positive changes and had some gratitude for the wake-up call regarding how the family spent their free time. My perception affected my opinion of my relative. Luckily, on the day I was calm enough not to lash out in anger or hurt pride. On another day, this could have happened. I am sure you can imagine how that situation would have played out.

We all meet people who are genuinely difficult to get along with. People have moods, disorders, physical ailments, or other personal challenges that affect their interactions with others. How do we deal with people who are genuinely cantankerous and disagreeable? Perhaps even potentially violent and aggressive?

Such situations usually fall into roughly two broad camps:

First, acute situations. We are face-to-face with someone unpleasant, rude, aggressive, or worse. You might find yourself in an acute situation because of your job. I know I have. You might be in a job where you must deal with the public regularly or you might be at the front line of service delivery and something has gone wrong. Sadly, you might be in a domestic situation in which you are subjected to unreasonable behaviour. If this is the case, you need to make changes for your safety and well-being. No one should live with fear or threat at home. Our home should be our refuge and sanctuary.

Second, we have chronic situations. These could be more low level in terms of drama but can be wearing and emotionally draining. This could be because of relatives we feel we have a duty to see, or a neighbour or colleague that we can't avoid.

So how do we lessen our stress and anxiety in dealing with people we consider being difficult, stressful, or anxiety-provoking? How do you handle rudeness, aggressiveness, or unreasonable behaviour?

When we are in a situation of having to deal with someone who is being aggressive or challenging, we must consider our safety first. If your job exposes you to people who exhibit this behaviour, your company should have policies and procedures in place to guide and protect you. You should expect training in techniques to deal with such behaviour.

Mindfulness has a huge role to play in ensuring your optimal emotional health and well-being, to deal positively with such behaviours. The training given for jobs in which staff are routinely required to deal with challenging behaviour often focuses on de-escalation techniques. This means calming the whole situation down. It also means being aware of one's posture, stance, tone of voice, and facial expression. Not being aware of these aspects of our demeanour could turn a volatile but containable situation into a tragedy. Being mindful of our breathing, planting our feet firmly on the ground, keeping our expression kind, and behaving warmly and compassionately could defuse an emotionally explosive situation.

Having a regular mindfulness practice ensures that you are acting from a firm, steady base of calm. If you have a job that involves dealing with challenging people, it is essential that not only do you develop techniques to keep calm in a crisis but that you use techniques such as mindful relaxation, mindful movement, gratitude, self-care, and meditation to help process stressful feelings and manage anxiety about these difficult encounters in your work. Consistent mindfulness practice helps deal with the stress that builds up over time in challenging professions and will build resilience. Being aware of how your body feels, the breath, keeping a relaxed facial expression, and using guided meditations all help to re-resource. Highly stressful environments or contexts such as emergency service jobs, front-line care work, or prison service jobs can deplete emotional reserves and end up in burnout, stress, anxiety, and ill-health.

The second broad area in which we might have to deal with troublesome people is the ongoing low level 'stone in the shoe' type irritations, caused by people who are not particularly aggressive but who grate on our nerves. Remember, our perceptions can be very malleable. What we find irritating on one day, we might not even notice on another day. This underlines the need for self-care and the use of the practices outlined in this book. If we are feeling calm and have a compassionate view of ourselves and the world, irritations can seem less intense. The elderly lady in front of us in the supermarket queue slowly counting out her pennies could irritate, *or* it could be a reminder to us to slow down, breathe, and be grateful for our health. We might even offer to help. Extending such kindnesses can help not just the other person but also ourselves.

What should we do about people in our lives who appear to be rude or abrasive? Perhaps an overbearing older relative constantly giving you unsolicited advice. Or maybe a colleague who can be difficult: the gossiper, the bully, the know-it-all, or the complainer. Feeling at ease and comfortable in our own skin is the first step in managing our encounters with such people. If we are operating from a calm centre, people with agendas that are unhealthy or damaging have a tougher time affecting us. Their tactics can bounce off us and we move on with our day. We develop this calm centre by having a regular and well-rooted mindfulness practice. By fostering a compassionate and gentle approach, we might see past the petty behaviour of a colleague. Often, over time, you will see situations play out. I know I have. Sometimes I just don't have all the information about a person to put their behaviour into context. Then over time, I realize what it has been about all along, and I get an 'ah-ha' moment. It all fits into place.

By maintaining dignity, calm, and compassion in situations, we can avoid getting caught up in other people's drama. If there is a situation in which you feel bullied or persecuted, take action to seek support.

Practising compassion doesn't give others the right to mistreat us. We can bring compassion to a situation without being a walk-over. Anxiety can lead us to over-explain, over-apologise, or accept unacceptable behaviour. You have a right to be treated with respect and dignity. If you are dealing with someone who routinely is rude, abusive, or dismissive of your feelings, set your boundaries with a sense of compassion for them and you. If you are mindfully doing this, you will act with good intentions and in a dignified manner. If you need to stop seeing someone or limit contact, do it mindfully – but do it.

So, in summary, in dealing with people whom we find difficult, we need to take care of ourselves. If we are well-grounded and calm, we are in a better position to avoid being irritated or disturbed by the behaviour of others. If we are exposed to genuinely unreasonable people, techniques such as awareness of breath, slowing and deepening the breath, keeping a relaxed, mindful focus on the present moment, and detaching from our own strong emotional reactions can help us deal with situations that are acute or chronic. Taking such a mind-set can help not just in the moment but also in how we handle the stress and anxiety that such interactions can provoke in the longer term.

When life gets too frantic, it is so easy to think if we just go faster, work harder, get up earlier, make more effort, and push ourselves to the limit, we will succeed. In the short term, all these mammoth efforts might get you through an intense period of demanding work or a family crisis, but such huge personal sacrifices of effort and stress are unsustainable in the long run. If you must push yourself harder every day just to keep going or keep up with a job, re-evaluate your situation. Will you be able to keep this up?

If you think you can, what will the cost be in terms of health and well-being? So, look for mindful solutions and practise self-compassion and self-care. Ask for help and plan to make any necessary changes to feel more peaceful and content about your life.

You have the tools to not only get through a challenging period but also to thrive. By now, you will be familiar with some mindfulness practices and techniques. I hope you have tried a few and experienced their benefits. Also, you will now be familiar with some attitudes of mindfulness: compassion, gratitude, non-judging, acceptance, trust, letting go, patience, trust, and non-striving. By moving through a crisis or challenge mindfully, there is the opportunity to grow and learn from the experience. This can ease the strain of the experience and hasten your recovery from any negative consequences.

***

Many people worry that if they just accept their feelings or themselves as they are, they will become unmotivated and resigned. This is a mistake. I will explain, using parenting as an example. If a child makes a mistake or does badly in an exam at school, a parent might react in one of three ways: they might scold the child and call them nasty names, threatening them with punishment if they don't improve, the child might work harder, or they might just give up. Most people would agree that this type of motivation comes at a big cost to the child's mental and emotional health. Another approach might be for the parent to say something like,

"Everyone fails sometimes. I love you as you are. Don't worry about exams." This might seem compassionate, but it will not help the child to do well in life. A truly compassionate approach would be to motivate and support the child by saying something along these lines: "I love you anyway, but I want you to do well and succeed in life. So, let's work out how to do better next time. We could talk to your teachers or get you some extra tuition." This response is motivating the child in a kind and supportive way.

If you want to change an aspect of yourself in some way – whether physical health, thinking, or behaviour – speak to yourself as a loving parent would to a child. Encourage and support yourself. Act like a wise and kind coach who will cheer you on. Look for helpful techniques to improve and celebrate success. Compassion can be very motivating and encouraging. Shame might work in the short-term, but it is not sustainable and will eat away at self-esteem and self-worth.

Help yourself by preparing as best you can for difficulties life might throw at you. This is a compassionate act of self-care. These preparations help in two ways. Firstly, you will be doing what you can to ensure problems can be dealt with, minimising any negative impact they might have on you. Secondly, you will be freeing yourself from any nagging, background worry that is troubling you. You can prepare as best you can and then let the concern go. When a storm in life hits, it can come unexpectedly in the form of a loss, sudden bereavement, or illness. Sometimes we might have some warning – such as when we know we will have an intensely busy period at work coming up, or we are starting a new job, or moving to a new house – in which case, we can prepare. For example, looking after your finances and saving a little each month can provide a cushion if there is an emergency or a loss of income. Being responsible about your finances is an act of self-care and compassion. Other preparations can be specific or general. If you know in some detail what to expect, you can make more specific preparations. If you have a well-established mindfulness practice, this will help prepare you for the unexpected demands life might throw our way.

Being mindful in the present doesn't mean we can't plan. By setting aside some time to prepare, we can free up our mental and emotional space to be fully present now. We need not worry or ruminate about the future, as we have done our best to make any necessary preparations. By doing this, we are making things easier for ourselves in the longer term.

To ease the stress of difficult life events, you can prepare and plan as best you can with presence and patience. This could mean asking for help, easing up on other commitments, or making peace with yourself by lowering your expectations in some areas. Avoid perfectionism and focus on making tasks easier, not more complicated. Do whatever you can on a practical level to help you get through a demanding time with minimum anxiety or stress.

Plan what you will do to get through, including having an established mindfulness practice. This does not have to be complicated or time-consuming. Take a few moments in the morning for a short meditation or reflection on a mindfulness attitude, remembering to check in with yourself at points during the day. Perhaps keep a pebble in your pocket to remind yourself – each time you feel the pebble, you could do a brief body scan, or deliberately slow your breathing and bring your mind to the present moment. You could physically ground yourself by saying something like: 'Feel your feet.' Plan for some resourcing or self-care activities. Ensure your schedule allows for adequate sleep and that you will eat nutritiously and stay hydrated. By having a plan and a routine you will avoid rushing, making poor, last-minute choices, and getting into the cycle of stress and anxiety. Remember to ask for help.

During periods of intense work, worry, or stress, it is easy to get caught up in a whirl of anxious thoughts, ruminations about the past future, self-doubt, and feelings of overwhelm. Break the stress response by being fully present in each moment. Be aware of the nuances of your feelings and sensations and take regular breaks. Remind yourself in times of increasing distress that, in this moment, all is well. If you feel anxious, stop and look around: is there a dire problem in this moment that must be dealt with right now? Probably not. Remind yourself that in that moment, you do not have a problem. Be present to the pleasurable things in life too. Enjoy what makes you feel good. Be fully present to everything you are experiencing. If you have intense feelings, bring your attention to the body, and breathe through them. Ground yourself and take comfort in knowing that you have prepared for this as best you can and surrender stressful feelings.

Know that this situation will pass. Life is constantly changing and unfolding. Do what you can to deal with your circumstances or feelings with as much presence of mind as possible. When you feel wearied by it all, know that it will move forward. Let the situation unfold and be patient and present to the experience.

To underline the benefits of compassionate preparation and planning, I would like to refer to the analogy of getting caught in a riptide. With some preparation such as checking the weather forecast, beach safety alerts, and tides, we would avoid ever getting caught in a riptide, if we ever *do* get caught in a riptide, we will be able to act quickly and effectively because we have a plan and know what to do. If one gets caught in a riptide, the best advice is to go with the current. Don't fight or struggle against it. Stay calm, breathe, and be present. Shout and wave ask for help but don't resist the current, you will only exhaust yourself and get nowhere.

***

Now, I would like you to take a moment to recall any potential future scenarios in your life that makes you feel anxious. Don't focus on the emotion around these situations – write them all down. List all the situations that make you feel worried. Now pick one, ideally one situation that causes you to feel uneasy but is not overwhelming. Something easy. What you are going to do is list all the things you can do now to make it easier *if* it did happen. For example. My husband would get very anxious about losing his mobile phone, and for good reason: he does all his banking on the phone, all his contacts details are listed in the phone, and it contains a huge amount of personal information, photos, and documents that, if lost, would cause serious inconvenience and worry. He would go into a mild panic if he thought he had lost the phone. I got used to his habit of frantically patting his pockets and looking around anxiously for the phone. Eventually, he arranged for some software to back up the phone and now has a plan about exactly what to do to help him locate and disable the phone in the event of it being lost or stolen. No more panicky pocket patting.

So, write down what you can do to help in a situation that makes you feel worried or anxious. It does not matter if it probably will never happen, by planning you will free up mental space that is being taken up with worry and rumination about this possible event. Once you have written down what you can do and you take some action, let it go. You have done what you can do for now and you will be in a better position if this possible situation ever did happen.

***

I will close this chapter with a short loving-kindness meditation:

May I be happy.

May I be safe.

May I be healthy, peaceful, and strong.

May you be happy.

May you be safe.

May you be healthy, peaceful, and strong.

Spend a few moments now quietly reflecting on how you feel as you say the words of this loving kindness meditation slowly. You could use this meditation if you are troubled by thoughts of a situation or person who has upset you.

Being compassionate does not take up much more time than not being compassionate, so adopt compassion as a constant companion as you go through each day. Just having the intention of being kinder and gentler on yourself is practising self-compassion. Keep it as a personal compass to help put you back on track when you feel irritation, criticism, or slip into unrealistic expectations of yourself or others. You will be calmer and happier for it.

Meditation 7: Compassion.

Settle yourself into a comfortable lying or sitting position with a straight spine. Close your eyes and bring your awareness to the breath. Just observe the breath. Be aware of how fast or slow you are breathing. Take notice of how deeply you are breathing. Deepen the breath. Be conscious of the abdomen inflating and, without undue exertion, bring the breath right the way down into the lower belly. As you exhale consciously slow the breath down, breathing out through the nose. As you do so, feel any tension slipping away from your shoulders. Relax the jaw by dropping the jaw slightly.

On the next out-breath, relax the chest and abdomen. Feel a sense of looseness in the whole torso, head, and neck. Breathe in deeply and, as you breathe out, focus on releasing any tension in the arms and hands. Relax the fingers, allowing them to go limp with a natural curl of the fingers inwards towards the palms. Now bring the attention to the buttocks, hips, and thighs. As you breathe out, allow this area to relax. Have a sense of being grounded in this part of the body as you sit or lie. Feel a sense of heaviness here that helps this area sink more deeply into the surface that is supporting you.

Bring your attention down your legs into the feet. Notice any sensations around the feet. Or notice any lack of sensation around the feet.

Sit for a few moments, aware of the entire body as you lie or sit.

After a few moments, bring your attention back to the area around the chest. Focus on the heart. Keep your focus on the heart and chest area as you breathe gently, deeply, and steadily. Put your right hand over your heart and breathe into it. Perhaps you are aware of the beating of the heart. Sit with the breath for a few moments.

Bring to mind the thought that all humans and sentient beings have a heart. A heart and mind that feels all the range of emotions you feel. Have a sense of gentleness and compassion for yourself. Focus on your own heart and as you continue to breathe in and out, breathe in the word 'kindness' and breathe out 'compassion'.

Direct this kindness and compassion towards yourself. Then, after a few breaths, consider the people in the room or dwelling you are in. Direct the kindness and compassion towards them. Continue in this way, considering people in your local community, even people you don't know. Include all living beings as you wish. Radiate your focus out to include all people in your town or city. Then all people in your country and so on. Eventually, moving your consciousness out to include everyone on the continent you live on and then the whole globe. If you lose focus, just bring the attention back to the breath and the heart area.

Sit with this focus for a few moments. Breathing in: 'kindness' and breathing out: 'compassion'.

Now let the breath settle into its usual pattern. Just notice how you feel. Do this without judgement.

After a few moments, deepen the breath. Stretch your arms up and allow for a refreshing stretch.

Stand up slowly and carry on with your activities with an attitude of kindness and compassion for all beings.

Chapter Eight: Continuing the Journey.

*"The real chapter eight is the rest of our lives!"
– Jon Kabat-Zinn.*

***

Louise looked around at the participants on her evening course. Vikki caught her eye and winked. This was the last week of the course and Louise realized she would miss attending it. After this brief lapse of concentration, Louise brought her attention back to what the course leader was saying. "If anyone is interested, we will continue with an informal group each week to share teachings, meditate, and share experiences – would anyone be interested?" Along with a few others, Louise nodded enthusiastically.

This little group had helped Louise see that life wasn't quite as scary as she thought and that her constant worry habit was her main problem. People really listened to each other in the group and gave Louise time to speak up. This had helped her to verbalize her worries and feelings of inadequacy. Much to her surprise, many people shared similar thoughts about themselves, even Vikki.

Louise had got to know a few people well and looked forward to continuing to see them each week in an informal group. Louise realized that this was probably the first time she had ever genuinely wanted to join in anything with other people. The loneliness she had felt for so long eased.

***

Having just completed his first week in a new job, Rob closed the front door behind him and put the kettle on. He reflected on his week: it had been a busy one getting to grips with his new responsibilities, but he looked back on it with some satisfaction. He took a moment as he waited on the kettle to boil to feel gratitude for his new role as a car valet. It gave him a sense of satisfaction to polish up the cars and eased his money worries.

He made his tea and sat by the window enjoying the late afternoon sunshine. Out of habit he found himself checking his phone to see if he had any missed calls from his mother. The doctor had arranged a home care service for her, and Rob remembered she would have a carer visit her about now to help her prepare her evening meal, so of course she would be too busy chatting with the carer to bother him. Time was getting on, he had agreed to meet some friends for a game of darts and a beer at his local, so he needed to get a move on. It would be great to see his friends again, and tonight he would have something to talk about and a bit of money in his pocket. Life felt good.

***

I hope that his book has given you some hope that feelings of anxiety, stress, or overwhelm can be eased and that life can get better. Just taking a few small steps each day will have a cumulative effect and over time, with gentle and consistent effort, you will feel calmer and be able to deal with any issues that are causing you pain. Remember you do not have to this alone. Ensure you get support from friends, family, support group members or from a health professional.

Like any real-life journey, sometimes everything goes smoothly and at other times we come up against roadblocks. I hope the journey has gone smoothly for you. In this last chapter we will look at ways of staying on course with your mindfulness practice, what to do if you take a sudden dip back into feelings of acute anxiety, and how to develop your mindfulness practice.

If you are returning to this chapter because of acute feelings of stress or anxiety, begin this chapter's seven-day plan as soon as you can. Don't be tempted to think 'I am too stressed, busy, or anxious to start.' That's when you need it most. All you need to do is to set aside five minutes in the morning, five minutes at lunchtime, and five minutes in the evening for your mindfulness practice. We will look at the details of the plan later in this chapter.

The hardest thing about mindfulness is *remembering* to practise it, especially when we get caught up in the rush of life. However, everyday tasks and activities are opportunities to be mindful. Keep the following prompts in mind as you go through your daily routine. Don't worry about doing them all but keep your intention to be mindful in the forefront of your mind and bring attitudes of mindfulness to your daily routine in a general way.

On waking, focus on what you are grateful for, and set an intention for that day. This could be to be more compassionate or patient with others and yourself. This is easier said than done, especially if you have young children or pets to attend to first thing in the morning. You might feel compelled to check your phone or emails as soon as you open your eyes, and it is easy to get pulled into the busy-ness of the day as you wake up. You could try keeping an item on your bedside table that will be a reminder to begin your day mindfully. This could be a crystal, shell, or inspiring picture. If you must attend to the needs of children or animals, you can do this mindfully. Talk to them with compassion, respond to their needs with patience, and have gratitude for their presence in your life. If there are difficulties such as dealing with a toddler's wet bed or your dog barking, deal with the practicalities with acceptance and the knowledge that this situation will pass. Even if you just have a few seconds to yourself when you wake up, this is enough time to set an intention such as 'I will treat myself and others with compassion today.' Or 'I will focus on breathing well today as I go about my daily tasks.' Keeping it simple and brief will work best.

If you forget to set your intention in the morning, remember you can re-start your day at any time. If you suddenly remember later in the day, or are aware of anxiety or stress building up and you realize you have forgotten, you can take a few seconds to breathe, compose yourself, and set an intention for the rest of the day.

At regular points during the day, bring your awareness to your posture. Stand or sit up tall and be aware of the points of contact your body makes with the floor or surface supporting you. Consciously bring the shoulders down away from the ears and allow the ribcage to expand. Holding yourself erect will allow the breath to flow freely through the body. Perform an informal body scan often and ask yourself how you are feeling or what do you need. This helps avoid tension or anxiety building up, as you will become more aware of the nuances of your bodily sensation before they become too dramatic or overwhelming. By standing or sitting up tall you are also gently asserting your right to your space – no need to hide away or slouch around apologetically. See good posture as a way of treating yourself with dignity and compassion.

Make it a routine habit to regularly tune into the sounds around you. Bring your awareness to sounds far away and those close to you. Practice listening to sounds without making judgements or forming opinions about them.

As you go about your daily activities, remember to bring your attention to your breath, especially if you are beginning to feel perturbed or distressed. Slow down your breathing and just focus on the breath. You can hold an awareness and acceptance of any other thoughts or sensations, but if you find they are triggering you to feel anxious, keep your focus on the breath and the thoughts or feelings will gradually reduce and disappear as you will not be giving them any attention.

Eating and drinking are everyday pleasures during which we can practice gratitude and appreciation. Make time to eat and drink with full attention on the activity, away from screens or other distractions. If you are sharing a meal, keep your attention on the food and on the people in your company.

Walking, whether as a function to get from one place to another or for leisure, is an opportunity to tune into your bodily sensations, on what is going on around you, and to practice gratitude. Even if you are incredibly busy, you will need to walk somewhere, even if inside an office building or place of work. You can still walk briskly but avoid getting carried away with automatic thoughts that can induce anxiety or stress. Keep your focus on your surroundings and your physical sensations.

Standing in line or waiting is a chance to ground yourself – be aware of your feet on the ground and stand tall. Look around you and focus on the present moment. Feeling stressed, rushed, or impatient will not make the line move any faster, so you might settle into a sense of stillness as you observe what is going on around you or perhaps make conversation with someone else who is waiting. In that interaction, you can bring attitudes of mindfulness.

In your daily interactions with others, give the other person your complete attention and be present for them. Really listen to them without being distracted by your phone or electronics. How often do you find yourself 'listening' to someone when your mind is taken up with thinking what you will say back or drifts off to something else? If you notice this, don't judge yourself with harshness, but do congratulate yourself on noticing it and set an intention to listen with more focused attention.

And lastly, before sleep, practice gratitude for what you have appreciated about your day and reflect on how you have acted in line with your intention for that day. If you feel you have not behaved as you would have liked, practice self-compassion and think of ways to make it easier for yourself tomorrow to act in ways that are consistent with your intentions.

This might seem like a lot to remember but by simply setting an intention to complete daily tasks and activities as mindfully as you can, you will approach an increasing number of activities with a mindful attitude as this becomes more ingrained in how you operate. This means totally concentrating on what you are doing and giving the task in hand your complete attention. Engage all your senses in each activity and be curious about how you approach the task. Notice if you are rushing it or are you putting off getting started. You may find time flies when you are engaged in it and you enjoy it. The answers to these questions give you useful information about what is motivating for you. And what might be causing you stress.

Your journey into mindfulness so far has probably has not been perfect. You may have slipped up. You may have forgotten lots that you have read or missed out on practices I suggested. That is to be expected. Permit yourself to be human. The practices are there to help and support you. They are not meant as a straight jacket to restrict you or a tool of self-flagellation or punishment. Often, people with anxiety issues have a mind-set of perfectionism. They bring this perfectionism to their mindfulness practice and use their 'failure' as something else to beat themselves up with. Don't let this happen to you. Just do what you can.

If you feel you have gone off course, well done on seeing this in yourself. If someone else has pointed it out, thank them for the feedback. When you are in a calm and peaceful state, you can always reflect on the validity of other people's perceptions, but you are better doing this from a centred space rather than reacting in haste.

If you have an awareness that you are slipping back into the old stress response or feeling and acting anxiously, just stop and observe yourself. Be fully present to what you are feeling. Put your hand on your heart and have a sense of self-compassion. Keep doing this until you feel calmer.

***

"Weave your parachute every day, rather than leave it to the time you have to jump out of the plane." – Jon Kabat-Zinn

***

Daily, keep in mind a range of attitudes of mindfulness discussed throughout this book:

- Non-judging.
- Compassion.
- Acceptance.
- Letting go.
- Patience.
- Non-striving.
- Gratitude.
- Willingness.

These are attitudes to take into life each day. Now pause as you are reading this book and run a personal inventory. Then, with compassion, weigh up how you are doing. By that, I mean go back through the list of attitudes and reflect on how much they are part of how you relate to yourself and others. Do they show up in self-talk, in your behaviour and in your responses to other people, or life events? Take stock with as little emotion as possible. If you feel any sense of anger or impatience with yourself, be aware of it but don't dwell on it. Pick out a couple of attitudes and focus on them over the next couple of days. Take small steps. Don't rush or force anything. Let life unfold and be fully present in each moment.

If you feel that you have seriously gone off course and are feeling anxious or overwhelmed, look at some practical aspects too. We are biological as well as psychological beings, with physical needs that need to be attended to. So, ask yourself at regular intervals: What do I need? Feeling dizzy or faint might be due to low blood sugar, so get something to eat. If you feel overwhelmed, stressed, or have brain fog, you might need to take a break or have a nap. A useful acronym to remember four basic questions to ask yourself is: HALT: Ask yourself, are you:

>   Hungry?
>   Angry?
>   Lonely?
>   Tired?

Be aware of your feelings and emotions. Attend to your needs. Do these practical things first, then decide how to deal with what is making you feel anxious. For example, if you feel worried about going to work on a Monday morning, reflect on your routine. Can you ready yourself for Mondays by ensuring you have everything ready the evening before and have made any necessary preparations, such as assembling papers in your work bag? Rather than seeing these as tedious tasks that eat into your weekend, see these preparations as an act of self-care. You will be making Monday mornings less stressful. Allow yourself plenty of time in the morning to have breakfast and do all you need to start your day calmly. It can be tempting to push the snooze button on the alarm or spend an extra 20 minutes in bed scrolling through your phone but allowing yourself more time to get ready is much more caring towards yourself than an extra few minutes in bed. So, take some mindful action to take adjust your habits in the aspects of life you can control to avoid anxiety or overwhelm.

***

The following is a check-point list of some tools of mindfulness to reflect on. Look at the list and consider if you are using them, how often, and in what ways. If you realize you are not doing any or some of them, simply adjust your behaviour without self-reproach.

- Regularly take a moment to be aware of how you feel in your body and move gently to relieve tension. If you find it difficult to remember, set an alarm on your phone or PC and do it once an hour.
- Slow down your movements, breathing, and speech.
- Listen to a guided meditation.
- Consider your daily routine. Build-in some mindfulness practices and routines such as a body scan, sitting in silence, a mindfulness walk, or a guided meditation. Include opportunities for self-care and commit to doing at least one a day.
- Use your journal: pour out your feelings onto paper, write a plan for the day, and a plan for tackling the main issue or problem on your mind. Write down all your anxious thoughts and try to let them go.
- Ask for help. Talk to someone. Share your feelings and worries.

- Be compassionate and present for yourself and others – kind thoughts, words, and actions.
- Be intentional in how you spend your time and attention. Do activities that are nourishing and nurturing for yourself.
- Think about who you spend the most time with. What impact is this having on you?
- Look at your self-talk – is it critical and harsh? Try to use kinder words to yourself.
- Have a growth mind-set, which means learning from mistakes and moving on.
- Are you living in the past? Commit to being fully present today, minute by minute.
- Revisit the attitudes for mindfulness and take a stock of how you are applying these in your life.
- Let go of anything that is not serving you.
- Look at your home and work environments. Can you make them more calming?
- At the very least, make sure your bedroom is an oasis of calm and quiet. Avoid having a television or computer in your bedroom and don't work in bed.
- Write down three things you are grateful for in your life.
- Look at your diet and check how much caffeine or alcohol you are consuming. Is this contributing to your anxious feelings?

- Look at what you are mentally consuming – horror movies, thrillers, dark psychological novels, endless news reports. Cut down on anything disturbing or shocking. This is an assault on your nervous system.
- Try to keep your evenings calm and quiet.
- If you feel you need to make any major changes in your life, write down how you will do it, discuss it with someone you trust, and do what you can to make it happen.

If you feel you are doing well, enjoying life and you have embedded the practices into your life, well done! You can return to this list if you need to, as a quick reminder of points to check if you begin to feel unduly anxious or stressed. Later in the chapter we will look at how to develop your mindfulness practice but before we do that, we will look at a seven-day plan to cope in a period of more acute anxiety or stress.

***

A Seven-Day Plan.

This Seven Day Plan is intended to be used as a re-set if you feel that your mindfulness practice has slipped, and you are bothered by distressing anxiety or stress. Begin this with a clear intention to treat yourself kindly. Remember you cannot shame yourself into feeling calmer.

The plan for each day is:

- In the morning, listen to the short, guided meditation designed for periods of acute stress or anxiety. This meditation is the last meditation in this book and is contained in the next section.
- In the middle of the day, have a short break to go for a short walk. Breathe well and use all five senses to be fully aware of what the present brings in that moment.
- In the evening, write down three things you are grateful for that day. If you can think of more, write them down.

Link each of these activities to a prompt in your routine. For example, if you use putting the kettle on or setting up your coffee machine as the prompt to do the short meditation in the morning, you will have an improved chance of remembering to do it. Go for a short walk as soon as you have eaten lunch. In the evening if you take a bath or shower, perhaps use this as the prompt to get your journal out when you get into your pyjamas or dressing gown.

Keep the attitude of compassion foremost in your mind. Even just having the intention of treating yourself with compassion will help. Just decide to treat yourself more kindly. Observe all your thoughts, actions, reactions, and mistakes through the lens of compassion.

Commit to do this for seven days. Write the activities into your diary for each day, or on a calendar, or put reminders into your phone calendar. Give yourself some leeway with the timings and do what fits in with your routine. This could look like this:

7 am – Listen to a guided meditation.

Noon – Have a brief walk.

8 pm – Gratitude journal.

Remember, as a child, how you learned how to cross the road? You were probably told to stop, look, and listen. Keep this simple instruction in mind now.

You could even write the words STOP. LOOK. LISTEN on sticky notes and put them up in your car, your fridge, or on your computer. This is to help you remember to come back into the moment.

***

"Mindfulness isn't difficult. We just need to remember to do it." – Sharon Saltzberg.

***

Ask yourself small questions as you go through each day. For example: 'How am I feeling?' or 'Where am I feeling tension or upset in my body?' Look for opportunities to be of service or act kindly towards others. Be curious. If an event or person causes you any upset, ask yourself 'I wonder why this has upset me. Can I learn any lessons from this?'

You need not do everything suggested in this book. Small, comfortable changes will be more sustainable than a dramatic overhaul of your entire life that makes you feel overwhelmed and exhausted. Easy does it. Changing our lives takes time, effort, and consistency. Be gentle with yourself if you go off track. If you do, bring your awareness to the present moment and set aside some time to review a chapter or two in this book to help you get back on track.

We need not strive or suffer to be mindful. By paying attention and being present, you can be alert to your own inner wisdom and guidance. You need not search it out. It has been there all along. Just gently, quietly, and consistently bring your attention back to your body, breath, and the present.

Just as we need to continually breathe in and out without special effort, we can continually practise mindfulness to live fully without undue worry and fear. Mindfulness is a continuous day-to-day practice. At the end of eight chapters, we do not graduate; we continue to learn and grow, mindfully.

You may have got to this chapter and feel that you would like to develop your mindfulness practice. For example, you might want to develop your meditation practice. I hope the guided meditations have helped you establish a regular practice of sitting still and focusing on your body and breath. If you have established this as a regular part of your routine, you may wish to begin to sit in silence for a few moments.

By now, I hope that you will not be discouraged if thoughts come into your mind. Your mind is not your enemy. Your mind is designed to have thoughts. By noticing thoughts, you are practising mindfulness. It is not possible to be completely free of thoughts, but it is possible to detach from the constant stream of thoughts coming into your mind, clamouring from attention. With practice the thoughts will quieten down and feel less demanding, but please don't be disheartened if you are aware of a rush of thoughts whirring around in your mind - feel encouraged that you are aware of this. Settle down and watch your thoughts come and go. Look on the thoughts as useful information. They show you what is going on in your life.

The trick is not to get caught up with them. Distance yourself from the emotion that you would usually attach to the thought. Look at it and let it drift off. Sit with a sense of curiosity. What will come up today? You are not striving for a mind clear of thoughts; you are an observer of your thoughts. Begin by setting aside just five minutes to sit in silence. You can increase the time as it gets easier for you.

Throughout the book, I have referred to a focus on the breath in guided meditations and the body scan. I have also encouraged you to slow down your breathing and to check that you are breathing fully as you go about your routine. Now, hopefully, you are feeling confident and relaxed about focusing on the breath. You could try some specific breathing exercises to extend your practise. There is a list of some exercises to try in the appendix.

You might not agree with all the suggestions made in this book. You might struggle to adopt some practices, attitudes, and techniques. If you feel resistance to some suggestions, all I ask is that you will try some. You need not do all of them and you need not do them perfectly to feel some benefit. Willingness is the key to effective change. The improvements might come slowly or quickly, but with a slight amount of effort and some planning, you will make some improvements in how you feel and respond to the demands of life.

Remind yourself frequently that you are good enough. By cultivating presence in your life, you realize who you are. By experiencing life as only you can experience it fully and with focus and attention, you will discover who you are already. Look on it as uncovering rather than seeking something out.

Have trust in the process. You can take some ideas I put forward in this book and tailor the techniques and suggested plans to fit your life and who you are. Do what you can and then let go. Trust that your levels of anxiety and stress will improve if you take some action and then let go and see what happens.

Life is continually unfolding. Do what you can and let it unfold. By taking small, consistent daily steps to act in ways that show care and compassion for yourself and others, you will be on a path that feels much more comfortable. Regularly check yourself for self-criticism or shame. If you genuinely feel you have fallen short in some area, gently resolve to do better and let the shame go. Also, get any help or support you need. You do not need to go it alone.

We cannot go anywhere without taking ourselves with us. Therefore, the time and effort you have spent reading this book and applying some techniques and suggestions will be time well spent. Look on it as an investment that will continually surprise and reward you in terms of self-awareness, feelings of contentment, peace, satisfaction, and freedom from unnecessary fear, anxiety, and stress.

Without peace of mind, what do we have?

With peace of mind, we are better equipped to deal with the challenge's life will inevitably produce and to embrace all the opportunities, experiences, beauty, and joy it offers. So, this investment in yourself will benefit you and all those you meet.

***

"Meditate. Live purely. Be quiet. Do your work with mastery. Like the moon, come out from behind the clouds. Shine!" – Buddha.

***

I hope you can shine and be who you truly are!

Meditation 8: Five-Minute Mindfulness Meditation.

I have designed this guided meditation to be listened to when you are feeling intensely anxious or stressed. You may feel you have no time to slow down. You may feel rushed and harassed. We need a mindfulness practice more than ever during these times. I urge you to be compassionate with yourself and give yourself the gift of just five minutes to slow down a little, let go of some tension, breathe, and take stock.

Find a comfortable place to sit. Allow yourself to settle back into an upright chair. Stay erect but relaxed. Have your feet planted firmly on the floor. Your hands can rest cradled in your lap, palms facing upwards. You may wish to close your eyes gently.

Allow for some space between your chin and chest. Perhaps lift the chin a little to create more space and a sense of openness. Be aware of any tension in the jaw. Let the jaw relax by dropping the lower jaw a little and making some space between the upper and lower sets of teeth, breathing through the nose, deepen the breath just a little. Expand the ribcage and allow the abdomen to rise.

If thoughts arise, let them go on the next out-breath. Quietly say to yourself: 'It's just a thought.'

As you breathe in, have a sense of space and expansion in the chest and abdomen. Focus on a sensation of openness and space. Allow the shoulders to drop a little and feel tension ease away.

Enjoy a few moments to appreciate this brief time to let go of tightness and constriction. Let the breath flow in and out easily and gently. Let any thoughts just float away on the next out-breath.

Just breathing, easily and gently. Observing thoughts that come and go. Making no attachment with any thought, just letting them drift off. Enjoying a sense of ease and calm. Look on yourself with compassion and kindness and accept all sensations and thoughts that might come to mind. Just gently let them go and return to the breath.

Now, deepen the breath. Rotate the head gently and slowly in a small circle. On the next in-breath, bring the shoulders up to the ears, and on the out-breath let them drop. Notice how your body feels now you have spent a few moments consciously letting go of tension and allowing yourself to have a few minutes of quiet.

On the next in-breath resolve to take this feeling of ease, self-compassion, and calm with you as you carry on with your day.

When you are ready, open your eyes, smile, and stand up slowly.

Go through your day with kindness and compassion for yourself and all those you meet today.

Appendix 1: A Brief History of Mindfulness.

It is unnecessary to know the details of the history of mindfulness to practise it. I include this outline of how mindfulness has come to the western world and gained such popularity to give some background information.

Nowadays, mindfulness is a non-religious form of meditation. One does not have to ascribe to any religious or philosophical belief to practise mindfulness in any of its forms. However, mindfulness does originally spring from religious practice.

The origins of mindfulness are difficult to disentangle from the history of meditation and yoga. It would appear that mindfulness has its origins in Eastern religion and philosophy, namely Buddhism and Hinduism, having its roots in the Vedic traditions. They share the texts which inform the practice and history of yoga with the origins of mindfulness; texts such as the *Bhagavad Gita*. People have been practising mindfulness for millennia.

They say Hinduism to be the oldest religion in the world. It is an eclectic religion that has developed from a mixture of different traditions, religions, and philosophies. The term 'Hinduism' was only established in the 1800s. The Vedic traditions, which form a solid foundation for Hinduism as it is understood today, dates back four thousand years to the Indus Valley (modern-day Pakistan).

The history of Buddhism is easier to trace. Buddhism dates back four to five thousand years B.C.E. Siddhartha Gautama, who became known as Buddha, found Buddhism. Hinduism would have informed his upbringing. Buddha aims to show his followers the path to enlightenment. In Buddhism, mindfulness (Sati) is considered the first step towards enlightenment.

There is an overlap between yoga and mindfulness. Bringing the awareness to the body, breath and the present moment is central to the practice of yoga. The phenomenal rise of yoga in the west in recent years corresponds with the growing popularity of mindfulness during the same period.

In recent years the biggest influence on bringing mindfulness to the west is Jon Kabat-Zinn. Jon Kabat-Zinn founded the Centre for Mindfulness at the University of Massachusetts Medical School and the Oasis Institute for Mindfulness-Based Professional and Educational Training. This is where Jon Kabat-Zinn developed his Mindfulness-Based Stress Reduction Program. Jon Kabat-Zinn studied under Thich Nhat-Hanh, a Buddhist monk and peace activist. Jon Kabat-Zinn integrated this Eastern foundation with Western Science. This link with Science has helped to establish the popularity of mindfulness in the West.

Aside from academic science, teachers, and writers such as Jack Kornfield founded the Insight Meditation Society in 1975, which has helped to make mindfulness-based meditation so widely known and accepted in the modern Western world.

Appendix 2: Mindful Movement.

Slow, gentle, easy movements can help soothe the nervous system and work off some energy generated by anxious thoughts and stressful emotions. Focusing on movements can help us centre ourselves in our bodies and build awareness of any tightness or tension that could cause problems if left unchecked. We spend so much time in our heads thinking, planning, rehearsing what we might say, creating lists, thinking about what we need to do and so on, it can provide welcome relief just to focus on gentle movements to get us out of our heads and into our bodies.

These movements and stretches are based on traditional yoga poses. They are restorative and restful. The aim is to calm the nervous system, mind, and emotions. This will stimulate the parasympathetic nervous system which will release hormones that will calm you and be of benefit to all systems in the body, especially the immune system.

Equipment and Clothing.

All you need is to wear comfortable clothes, be barefoot, and use a thick rug or mat to lie on, a small towel to roll up to put behind the knees or the neck if needed and a blanket if it is cool. A cushion or two would be useful too. You do not need any specialised equipment. If you have done no exercise for some time, or have any medical issues, check with your doctor before starting any movement plan. Move slowly and gently. Do not do these poses immediately after eating a large meal. Allow a couple of hours for the stomach to empty before practicing the following movements. After lying down, please get up slowly. Move in an area that is uncluttered with furniture and is free from trip hazards.

The Pose of a Child.

Benefits: Stretches the hips, thighs, and ankles, while relieving stress and fatigue. Gently stretches muscles in the back and relaxes the muscles in the front of the body.

Contraindications: Should be avoided by pregnant women, those with knee injuries, injury at the ankle, severe spondylitis, or infection in the stomach.

Come down onto the mat on all fours. Bring the hips back onto the heels and open the knees wide, stretch the arms forward with palms of the hands down on the mat. Bring the head down to rest the forehead on a cushion or you can bring the hands under your forehead if you do not need the cushion. You could also have the arms resting, forearms down on the mat, alongside your thighs. Another variation is to have the arms stretched out in front, with hands resting on the mat in front of you. Do what feels comfortable for you. Don't over-stretch. Stay down in the pose for a few minutes, breathing well. Make sure the knees are open wide to allow space for the belly to expand. Come back up gradually, sitting upright for a few minutes before attempting to stand up.

Seated Forward Fold.

Contraindications: Any recent injury to the hips, arms, shoulders, or ankles.

Benefits: A calming pose that soothes the nervous system and provides a stretch for the back. It is said to stimulate the urinary and reproductive systems.

Forward bends can be very relaxing and comforting. Sit on the mat with your back upright and your legs in front of you, feet flat on the floor. Have a bend in the legs. Take a breath in and on the out-breath bring your chest down towards your thighs. Don't try to keep your legs straight, especially if your hamstrings are tight. Bring your thighs up to meet your chest, bend the legs as much as you need to. If you can begin to straighten the legs but keep your chest close to the thighs. Play about with the movement, gradually straightening out the legs in front of you. Tuck the tummy in to make more space. Stop when you feel you need to and rest in the pose there. The aim is to feel a gentle stretch and release in the back. Don't strain. When you are resting in the pose, breathe into your back, imagining that the lungs are pushing out the back rather than feeling crowded in the chest cavity. Enjoy a sense of comfort and calm here for a few moments. Come back upright slowly. To make this a more restorative pose, you could tuck a cushion under the backs of the knees and have a cushion under your chest, on top of your thighs to allow yourself to relax completely into the pose.

Legs up the Wall.

Contraindications: Those with glaucoma or detached retinas and people with heart conditions should not practice inverted positions. Some people maintain that women should not practice inversions during menses.

Benefits: Can lower stress and anxiety. It is helpful for insomnia. This posture is very soothing for tired or aching legs, especially if you have been standing for a long time.

Place a mat or thick rug at the front of a chair or at the end of a bed. Lie down on the mat on your back and bring your legs up to form a ninety-degree angle with your body. Rest the legs on the seat of the chair or on the end of the bed. Lie back and enjoy the restful feeling. You can have your arms on the floor by your sides, or if it is comfortable for your shoulders, you can bring your arms up over your head resting on the floor behind your head.

Alternatively, you could rest your legs up a wall. Sit on a mat or rug sideways along a wall, have your hip as close to the wall as possible, swing your legs up to rest on the wall, adjust yourself to get your hamstrings and bottom as close to the wall as you can. Lie back with the legs resting up the wall.

Tree Pose.

Contraindications: Anyone with recent or chronic hips, knee, or ankle problems. Take care if your balance is poor and stand near to a wall for support.

Benefits: This is a balancing pose and can help with focus, memory, and concentration. The pose helps to strengthen the legs.

Stand upright on a mat or firm surface. Stand close to a wall that you can use for support if needed. Arms by the sides and feet planted firmly on the floor. This is best done with bare feet. Imagine a string pulling your head up towards the ceiling, pull in your navel to make a strong core. Have a sense of energy in the arms and spine. Bring your weight slightly over to one side and ground the foot on that side into the floor, spreading the toes. Gradually lift the opposite foot a little way up off the floor. Begin by crossing the lifted foot over the ankle of the supporting leg. If you are confident doing this, you can bring the lifted foot up to cross at the shin of the supporting leg. Do not cross the leg over the supporting knee, as this could compromise the knee. To help with balance, it can help to stare at a spot ahead of you. Use a supporting wall to help support you if needed. Sometimes just a fingertip on a wall can help with balance. Otherwise, you can bring your arms out to the side to create a sense of openness and space. In time and with practice you can bring your arms up above your head, hands joined in a prayer position or out to the side up above the head.

Cat/Cow Pose.

Contraindications: Anyone with shoulder or neck problems, weak wrists, and pregnant women should avoid doing this without the supervision of an experienced instructor.

Benefits: Warms the body, increases flexibility in the back, and opens the chest, encouraging good breathing. The movement stretches the back, torso, and neck.

Get onto your knees on a mat or rug. Have the hands down on the mat, palms facing down and fingers well spread out. Focus on putting your weight onto the area of the hand where the base of the index fingers meets the thumb. Have the knees about hip-width apart. The fronts of the feet are resting on the mat. Have a sense of space across the upper back and keep the shoulders down away from the ears. Take a breath in and arch the back up gently, spreading the shoulder blades, tucking in the tailbone, and bringing the chin in towards the chest. On the out-breath, let the back dip down, bringing the shoulder blades together, the head up and slightly back and bringing the tailbone up. Do this for three or four rounds and then rest in the pose of a child for a few moments and repeat if you wish.

Reclined Butterfly.

Contraindications: Knee injury, lower back pain

Benefits: Stretches the inner thighs, relaxes, and calms the nervous system, improves the external rotation of the hips.

Lying back on the mat, open your knees out to each side and bring the soles of the feet together. You could tuck a cushion under each knee for support if needed. You can have your arms by your side, out to each side, or above your head if your shoulders allow it. This allows for a sense of openness and space across the chest and allows for deep, restorative breathing. Spend a few minutes here, breathing well.

Standing Forward Fold

Contraindications: Recent or chronic problems with the back, hips, legs, or shoulders.

Benefits: Stretches the back, the backs of the legs, stimulates the parasympathetic nervous system, the endocrine system, and the urinary and reproductive systems.

Stand upright on the mat, feet hip-width apart, hands down by your sides. Take a breath in and stretch up with both arms. Have a bend in the knees, a deeper bend if you have tight hamstrings. As you fold forward, bring the chest down towards the thighs. Bring the hands down to either rest on the shins or bring them down towards the floor. If your hands don't reach the floor, have a thick book, or firm cushion to rest your hands on. Focus on elongating and stretching the back. Let the head hang forward to release the neck. Stay here for a couple of breaths and slowly curl back upwards to a standing position.

Corpse Pose

Contraindications: If there are back issues, put a bolster or rolled-up towel under the knees, if there is a reverse curve in the neck, put a small, rolled towel behind the neck. The body should be warm. If the room is chilly, cover yourself with a blanket.

Benefits: This is a good pose to finish with so you can relax into it. It lowers blood pressure and slows breathing. Muscles can relax and let go.

This is an ideal pose to finish a movement session. Lie down on the mat with your legs stretched out and your arms by your sides. Cover yourself with a blanket if the room is cold. If you have lower back issues put a towel behind the knees. Have some space between the legs and let the feet turn out to either side. Bring your arms away from the body. Allow the backs of the hands to rest on the mat, palms facing upwards. Let the shoulders relax back against the mat. Have some space between your chin and your chest. Relax the jaw. Relax the muscles in the face. Have a sense of openness and space across the front of the body. Enjoy a few moments of deep, refreshing breathing and relaxation.

Allow the muscles to go loose and limp. When you are ready, move the feet from side to side and wiggle the fingers and toes. Roll the head from side to side. Turn over onto your side and support your head with the crook of your arm. After a few moments, push up with the opposite hand into a seated position. Take a few breaths here and make your way back to standing, slowly, without rushing.

These are just a few gentle and restorative movements to help calm your nervous system and provide some gentle stretching which can be a release for tight, tense muscles.

If you are interested in going further, I would advise you to join a class instructed by an experienced teacher. Many teachers provide private one-to-one sessions. Practising stretching and breathing will be beneficial physically, emotionally, and mentally.

Appendix 3: Mindful Breathing.

When anxious and stressed the most important thing to remember is to breathe slowly through your nose.

If you just remember to breathe slowly through your nose, your anxiety will lessen. Many studies have proven this.

Patrick McKeown has spent the last twenty years researching and learning about the positive effects of nasal breathing. He has trained athletes and helped people with a range of respiratory and cardiovascular disorders to breathe easily and exercise safely. Nasal breathing has a wide-ranging effect, not least in calming the nervous system and getting oxygen to the cells more efficiently. Patrick McKeown has shown how the nose and diaphragm are connected and that nasal breathing helps the diaphragm work more efficiently. This allows the lungs to inflate fully.

You know you are using the diaphragm efficiently when your abdomen inflates. If your tummy stays flat and only your chest rises and falls, you are not breathing fully. This shallow chest breathing has been shown to exacerbate feelings of stress, panic, or anxiety. The diaphragm is a large muscle at the floor of the ribcage. When you breathe in fully, the diaphragm opens like an upside-down umbrella creating more space for the lungs to inflate with air. Like any muscle, the more you exercise it, the stronger it will become. A strong, well-toned diaphragm will help you have a stronger respiratory system. This has a host of beneficial health effects. If you are interested in this subject, Patrick McKeown has written an excellent book on the subject. Please see the details at the end of this section.

In moments of acute stress, it's difficult to recall complicated breathing exercises with set patterns of counting, and so on. It is best to practise the techniques suggested below when you feel calm. That way you will have a memory of what to do that you can call on when you become stressed or anxious. For some people, this will take time and practice. I have worked with some people who get stressed about breathing in a certain way and need this calm practice to build up their skills and confidence gradually. When you feel you have got the hang of the techniques, you can then use them when you need to.

The main takeaway here is to focus on breathing slowly through the nose when feeling acutely stressed. Try these techniques that follow, when you are feeling calm and see what works best for you. Keep a couple as a 'go-to' to use when you feel anxious or are preparing yourself for an event you know will probably trigger anxiety for you.

On a day-to-day basis, at points during the day, check your breathing;
are you breathing through the nose and deeply into the abdomen area? Are you breathing slowly? This will be a useful habit to adopt to avoid sensations of stress or anxiety due to inefficient breathing.

Equal breathing.

This means breathing in for the same length of time as you breathe out. Usually, the recommendation is to breathe in on a count of four and breathe out on a count of four. You can do this for as long as you need to feel calmer and more cantered.
Breathe in on a count of four, hold for a count of seven and breathe out on a count of eight.

On the first in-breath count one, breathe out on two, breathe in on three, breathe out on four and repeat counting from one to four, and coordinating the counts with the breath for as long as you need to.

Belly Breathing.

Lie down on your back, with legs bent and feet flat on the floor. Have your hands placed on your belly, Breath in deeply through the nose filling the belly up with air. Breathe out slowly through the nose. When you can do this comfortably and calmly on your back, you can practise it sitting or standing. In time you will be able to do this anywhere. When you can do this, you can go back to belly breathing lying down on your back but with a book or beanbag on your belly. You can practise lifting the book or beanbag using the breath and muscles in the belly. This is a great way of strengthening the respiratory system, especially for people who have cardiovascular issues or other health issues which limit the amount of cardiovascular exercise they can do safely.

The above are just some simple breathing exercises to try. Breath-work (or in yoga pranayama) is an amazing practice for both body and mind.

Further resources on breathing

McKeown, P., The Oxygen Advantage: Simple Scientifically Proven Breathing Techniques to Help You Become Healthier, Slimmer, Faster, and Fitter, 2015. Available on Amazon.

Appendix 4: Eating a Meal Mindfully.

The following are some guidelines on eating a meal mindfully. This is a wonderful practice that helps to slow us down, calm down the nervous system and aids good digestion and eating habits.

Avoid eating with other distractions going on. Switch off the television and do not have your phone or laptop on the table. Sit at a table in a comfortable upright position. Look at your meal and take a moment to feel or express gratitude for the food on your plate.

You could reflect on all the hard work it has taken to produce the food and get it onto your plate. Take a few deep breaths into the belly and notice how you feel.

Mindful eating is about engaging all our senses in the experience. Before you put any food in your mouth, appreciate the colours of the food. Notice any contrasting colours such as bright red tomatoes with sprinkles of vibrant green herbs. Breathe in the food's aroma with appreciation and anticipation.

As you eat, be aware of the texture of the food in your mouth. Is it chewy or soft? Are you craving a certain texture? Chew slowly, fully experiencing the flavours and textures of the food.

Put your fork down between bites. Take your time to enjoy the meal. Try to make the meal last for twenty minutes. This gives the body time to register that food has been ingested. Eat until you feel comfortably full but not overfull. Enjoy a sensation of satiation balanced with a comfortable sense of lightness. You do not want to feel overfull or stuffed.

Enjoy the meal and savour all the tastes, textures, and aromas as you eat. Notice how you feel physically and emotionally. Has your mood changed as you have eaten? This might seem a lot to remember. Practice what you can. Take your time and appreciate the meal. Try not to rush your food. Use all your senses and enjoy the food.

Appendix 5: Self-care Activities

Physical Well-Being.

- Movement (walking, jogging, horse-riding, yoga, dancing, cycling, swimming and so on.)
- Sleep and rest – including naps and good sleep hygiene.
- Food and hydration.
- Limits on alcohol/ junk food, etc.
- Limits on screen time.
- Massage.
- Haircut.
- Facial.
- Hot shave.

Intellectual

- Learning a language.
- Reading.
- Games.
- Quizzes.
- Teaching a skill.
- Learning a new skill.
- Skill swapping.
- Playing a sport that requires mental effort such as golf.
- Studying.
- Making instructional videos.

- Teaching a language or practising conversation with an additional language speaker.
- Setting work or career goals.
- Being a mentor or finding a mentor.
- Asking for feedback.
- Learning to play an instrument.
- Crafts.
- Art.
- Gardening.
- DI.Y.
- Decorating.
- Flower arranging.
- Sewing.
- Photography.
- Card making.
- Baking a cake.
- Carpentry.
- Writing poems or stories.
- Writing a song or piece of music.

Spiritual

- Getting out into nature.
- Reading inspirational books.
- Spiritual pursuits.
- Spending time with animals.
- Listening to talks, uplifting podcasts.
- Watching nature documentaries.

- Looking at the stars and moon.
- Looking up at the sky every day.

Social

- Ringing a friend or loved one.
- Writing a letter or card.
- Writing an email.
- Sending some photos.
- Hugging a loved one.
- Giving a small gift.
- Being present
- Joining a club/church/group.
- Starting or taking part in a self-help group. Voluntary work.
- Babysitting for a friend or relative.

Emotional

- Being present most of the time.
- Taking time out just to 'be'.
- Slowing down.
- Writing in a journal.
- Appreciating.
- Doing kind acts.
- Acknowledging emotions.

- Practising attitudes of mindfulness.
- Silence.
- Solitude/alone time.
- Hugging a loved one or a pet.

Personal

- Organising a closet or drawer.
- Cleaning and tidying.
- Washing the car.
- Being aware of finances and spending.
- Avoiding borrowing money.
- Budgeting.
- Setting financial goals.
- Writing realistic to-do lists.
- Keeping a diary/calendar.
- Arranging for some help if needed.
- Creating a collage or vision board.

Resources

BOOKS

- Eight Chapters to Optimum Health. A Proven Program for Taking Full Advantage of Your Body's Healing Power. Andrew Weil. Ballantine Books, 1998.
- Feeling Good. David Burns. William Morrow, 1980.
- Mindfulness in Plain English. Henepola Gunaratana. Wisdom, 1991.
- The Stress Solution. Dr Rangan Chatterjee, 2018.
- The Way of Zen. Alan Watts, 1999.
- The Mindful Way Through Depression. Mark Williams, John Teasdale, Zindel Segal, Jon Kabat-Zinn. The Guilford Press. 2007.
- The Seven Day Mental Diet. Emmet Fox. DeVorss, 1963.
- Stillness Speaks; Eckhart Tolle; Namaste Publishing; 2003.
- The Power of Now: Eckhart Tolle; Namaste Publishing; 1999.
- Yoga The Spirit and Practice of Moving into stillness; Erich Schiffmann; Simon and Schuster; 1996.
- Emotions: A 10-Day Plan to Overcome Stress, Anxiety and Negativity; Lewis David; Winspress; March 2020.

References

Chapter One

1. McGonigal, K. The Upside of Stress. Penguin, 2015.

2. Maguire, E.A., Spiers, H. & Woollet, K. "London Taxi Drivers and Bus Drivers: A Structural MRI and Neuropsychological Analysis". Article in Hippocampus 16(12):1091-101 (2006).

3. Wagner, A. Multi-Taskers Have Reduced Memory, 2018 (A discussion on this research can be found at https://news.stanford.edu/2018/10/25/decade-data-reveals-heavy-multitaskers-reduced-memory-psychologist-says/).

4. Rosen C. "The Myth of Multi-Tasking". Article in The New Atlantis 20 (12): 105-110 (2008).

Chapter Three

1. Cameron, J. The Artist's Way, Tarcher/Perrigree, 1992.

Chapter Four.

1. Beuttner, D. The Blue Zones of Happiness, National Geographic, 2017.

2. Lisle, D, and Goldhammer, A. The Pleasure Trap, Healthy Living Publications, 2003.

Chapter Five.

1. Ahearne, D., Farrant, K., Hickey, L. *et al.* Mindfulness-based stress reduction for medical students: optimising student satisfaction and engagement. BMC MED EDU. 16, 209, 2016.

Chapter Seven.

1. Brewer, J. A Simple Way to Break a Bad Habit TED Talk, 2016. (This talk can be found online at https://www.mindful.org/simple-way-break-bad-habit/)

2. Konrath, S., O' Brien, E. and Hsing, C. "Changes in dispositional empathy in "American college students over time: a meta-analysis," Sage Journals, August 2010.

3. Hamilton, D. The Five Side-Effects of Kindness, 2011

4. Bazarco, D., Cate, R., Azocar, F., et al. "The impact of an innovative mindfulness-based stress reduction program on the health and well-being of nurses employed in a corporate setting". <u>Journal of Workplace Behavioural Health</u>, 28 (2), 107, 2013.

Acknowledgements.

A huge thank you to my husband for his encouragement and support. Thank you to all the people who have helped me grow over the years – even if it was painful at the time. Thank you to all the lovely people who have attended my yoga or meditation classes; it has been an honour and privilege to be trusted by you all. Thank you to all my family and friends for your support, trust, and love.

About the Author.

Antonia Ryan grew up in Belfast, Northern Ireland. She obtained a BA in English and History from the Queen's University of Belfast and worked for Social Services in England, qualifying as a Social Worker and Practice Teacher in Social Work in the 1990s. Antonia has a Post Graduate Certificate in Education and has Qualified Teacher Status. She has worked mostly with children and young people with Social, Emotional, and Behavioural issues. She has post-graduate qualifications in Behavioural Psychology and Developmental Psychology. Antonia has also qualified as a Life Coach and as a certified Yoga Teacher. She has taught yoga and meditation to children, young people, and adults of all ages and backgrounds. She is married with four adult children. Antonia divides her time between Devon in the UK and Portugal. Her interests are yoga, meditation, walking, running, cooking, reading, and writing both fiction and non-fiction.

Printed in Great Britain
by Amazon